Leave Us Some Unreality

New Writing from the Oscar Wilde Centre,
Trinity College Dublin

Gibson Huntley Press

First published by Gibson Huntley Press 2010
Copyright © Gibson Huntley Press

The authors of *Leave Us Some Unreality* gratefully acknowledge
the generous financial support of the School of English, TCD.

ISBN-13: 978-0-9555025-9-0
ISBN-10: 0-9555025-9-4

Cover Photograph by Hannah Breslin
Cover design, text design and typesetting by Karen Carty of Anú Design
Printed and bound in Ireland by ßetaprint

Typesetting Font Bulmer

Leave Us Some Unreality
Oscar Wilde Centre for Irish Writing
21 Westland Row
School of English
Trinity College Dublin
Dublin 2
Republic of Ireland

For information about the book visit
www.leaveussomeunreality.wordpress.com

To contact the authors email
owc.anthology@gmail.com

For information on the M. Phil in Creative Writing, visit
www.tcd.ie/OWC

OSCAR WILDE

THE THIRTEEN CLUB

(*Times*, January 16, 1894.)

At a dinner of the Thirteen Club held at the Holborn Restaurant on January 13, 1894, the Chairman (Mr. Harry Furniss) announced that from Mr. Oscar Wilde the following letter had been received: –

I have to thank the members of your Club for their kind invitation, for which convey to them, I beg you, my sincere thanks. But I love superstitions. They are the colour element of thought and imagination. They are the opponents of common sense. Common sense is the enemy of romance. The aim of your Society seems to be dreadful. Leave us some unreality. Do not make us too offensively sane. I love dining out, but with a Society with so wicked an object as yours I cannot dine. I regret it. I am sure you will all be charming, but I could not come, though 13 is a lucky number.

Staff

Acknowledgments

The authors of *Leave Us Some Unreality* would like to thank: Gerald Dawe, Deirdre Madden, and Carlo Gébler for their guidance and encouragement; our lecturer and editorial advisor Jonathan Williams for his indispensable technical and creative advice; our writer fellow Molly McCloskey and Professor Richard Ford for inspiring us to write in new ways; Dr. Darryl Jones, Brenda Brooks and the School of English, Trinity College Dublin; The Long Room Hub; Drs. Eric and Karen Louie; Hannah Breslin for our cover photograph; Karen Carty of Anú Design for visual inspiration and layout; and Ray Lynn of ßetaprint for print management.

Special thanks to Lilian Foley for her indefatigable support and for making the Oscar Wilde Centre a home to us all. Finally, many thanks to everyone who helped and contributed towards this anthology.

Contents

Foreword

It was only in the nineteenth century that literary criticism became a taught subject within universities. Then in the twentieth century universities began to offer creative writing, and imported practicing writers to teach it. I'm a beneficiary of this development and the students whose work follows this are students I've known and taught. I believe in glasnost so you should also know I'm writing this because all the contributors here are writers (and people) I like.

The M. Phil in Creative Writing at the Oscar Wilde Centre in Trinity is a lovely thing. I'd love to do it myself. For a year the student writes and reads. It's intense, exciting, and it really does what a university course is supposed to do (but usually doesn't anymore because of the way the weasels who run our universities have arranged things): it catalyzes maturation, it tempers the student's mettle, and it educates.

However, writing and reading can only educate a student so far. It can get the student to complete a manuscript but for that work to be really finished it must be out in the world and in a reader's hands.

Many institutions help novices to write better but the M. Phil at the Oscar Wilde Centre does something very special because it gets their work from the completed to the finished stage.

Every year the M. Phil in Creative Writing students collectively produce, for commercial publication, an anthology of their work. They select the content, organise its sequencing, choose a type font, agree on a cover, pick a title and attend to all the many other things that have to be done in order to translate manuscript into publishable and published copy.

By the time they get to the end of the process (which prepares them for work in publishing should they ever wish to enter that profession) what they have is a proper book, with an ISBN and a retail price, which of course contains a piece of their work.

Though it's not necessary for writers to publish and though you can be a writer without publishing it's also true that the experience of seeing work you've made in print is a good thing. This, I believe, is because it's only when you see what you have made in print that you really see its worth and can then work out what you must do next.

It's also important, I think, to see something you've made in a form where you can't meddle with it any more. On one level nothing is ever finished because it's never perfect but everything can be got to the stage where it passes muster, and the only way to know that you can and must do this is to see your work in print.

The M. Phil class of 2009–2010 produced *Leave Us Some Unreality*. There were costs but the money they needed came from sales of the anthology produced by the class of 2008–2009. The profits generated by *Leave Us Some Unreality* will in turn support the anthology that the class of 2010–2011 will make. Our culture is stupid and wasteful but I'd exempt from that stricture the literary equivalent of the perpetual motion machine that is the Oscar Wilde Centre anthology.

And what of the content? Well, this will prosper. It deserves to. All the work here was made with care and attention: then it was sanded and smoothed, polished and burnished until it shone. "He's prejudiced," you're thinking. You're right. But the prejudiced can be right as well as being prejudiced.

Carlo Gébler

Monday, 22 March 2010

David Rowell

Jasper McGinity Goes to Trinity

At retirement age, it came to pass,
when others happily went to grass,
that, full of zeal and seeking knowledge,
Jasper applied to go to college.
He scanned the book-list for the year
and bought them all, cut back on beer.
In summertime, through Irish rain,
he read these tomes to tell his brain
that for the coming year he'd need
it working well, at increased speed.
His friends, who heard of his intention,
thought Jasper should enjoy his pension,
like them, by playing golf all day
or taking sun at San Tropez.
But Jasper stayed, with much *ésprit,*
in readiness for Trinity.

The day came, which he wanted most,
and after his boiled egg and toast
he kitted out and left the house
saying *adieu* to loving spouse.
He boarded the tram, that wasn't hard,
flashing his old-age pension card.
Saying goodbye to ordinary mortals
he tottered through the college portals,
anxious of mind and heart all fluttery
he steeled his nerve with buns at Buttery.
The waitress, noting this ancient dresser,

mistook him for an old professor,
she patted his arm and called him "*dear*,"
he wondered if he'd last the year.

Jasper's fears were nullified,
his class were warmth personified,
none of them seemed to worry about
his doddery feet and dripping snout.
The professors, being of the sagest,
knew that Trinity was never ageist,
to teach this fossil they'd no fears,
older than them by twenty years.

But Jasper proved himself no fool,
he cosied up to the Medical School.
They found his body strange indeed,
it was so decrepit and gone to seed,
and, much to Jasper's jubilation,
he starred in anatomy demonstration.
Before he knew it, they worked their arts
on his creaking and faulty body parts,
his joints and sinews were replaced
and his ribs in steel were all encased.
When this news reached the rugby patch,
they picked him for the Colours match,
and the UCD crowd turned and ran,
they couldn't beat the bionic man.

The Provost wanted someone new
to draft the College ten-year view,
the poor man himself was all confused
'til he read of Jasper in the *Trinity News*.
"*I have him at last,*" he said to the Board,
"*he'll do the trick, I give you my word.*"
These tidings brought the Board up short,
they got so excited they spilt their port.
The Provost ran to scout the place,
find Jasper quick, get face to face.
He looked in Berkeley and Ussher too,
the Pav and O'Neills to name but few,
just when he thought his quarry was missed
he found Jasper orating at the Hist,
he was for the motion, spoke for half an hour,
"*this house believes in eighty-year power.*"

Well you know the rest, so it won't take long
to top and tail this epic song,
of Jasper as Provost at eighty-five
still going strong, even more alive.
The moral of the story at the end of the dish:
if the writing's creative – say what you wish.

Island

I can't see you but I know you're there,
a compass bearing could not be more true
than my instinctive reckoning
of your constant shape.

I've seen you in myriad different lights,
clear like Hy Brasil, or Bali Hai,
sometimes just a hazy blur
peeping from the sea-mist at your base.

Today I am missing you since dawn.
The rain has cloaked the surface of the bay;
resigned, I crunch along the shingle beach,
the smell of seaweed strong above the tide.

A sudden lift – the evening sun
for a brief span wins the contest with the rain,
you emerge fresh and in triumphant dress
emerald set in vivid aquamarine.

Black Dog

Recession seems too bleak a word to say,
we lived our glorious lives without a care.
Things may be worse tomorrow than today.

Bankers who gave loans with proud display
now whisper and confess the coffers bare,
recession seems too bleak a word to say.

Venison and Chablis ruled. Dismay
now washes down dry bread. *Ma chère*,
things may be worse tomorrow than today.

New cars adorned the drive. They're gone away.
The bailiff came, now we're on Shanks mare.
Recession seems too bleak a word to say.

The month we spent each year in San Tropez
has dribbled to a wet weekend somewhere.
Things may be worse tomorrow than today.

Creditors at the door demanding pay,
our leaders look at us in blank despair.
Recession seems too bleak a word to say,
things may be worse tomorrow than today.

Solo

I clear the shelves of unread books.
Out of sorts from my betrayal,
old friends cast aside, I stride to town
determined to settle an uneasy mind.

In the morning air, I hear a violin,
perfect pitch, clear notes without
accompaniment, soar over rooftops,
the windless sky, like October leaves.

Tunnel

Brick walls and sealed doors
constrain the route,
no side exits or reliefs.
Nothing to bar a turning back,
but having come this far
it would be shameful to retreat,
better to face the oldest fears,
better to go on.

At the tunnel's end,
a heavy door slides open
releasing the smell of leather
and ancient paper.
The grave custodian,
with furrowed face, unblinking,
oblivious to the dry heat,
seeks an identity.

The volume is located,
it holds no secrets back,
yet reserves its position
against a hurried reading,
some pages still uncut.
Patience to peer obliquely
comes to seasoned eyes,
neck bent in the harsh light.

Relief comes in a cool rush,
a segment is in place.
The document is replaced,
the door unlocked,
the world's balm fills in
along the tunnel,
until a new demand
will force a return.

Catherine Finn

Maths Problem

It's raining and Mum is late again. Four red cars pass but none are Mum's. I wait at the school gates, standing under the horse chestnut tree. Fat brown conkers litter the path, as if it's been raining giant chocolate drops. More hang on the tree above me, warm and dry in their prickly green shells. I pull up my hood and move closer to the tree trunk.

Finally, Mum pulls in by the path and I get into the front seat. Daddy won't let me sit in the front. He says I'm too young; he says I can sit here when I'm twelve, but Mum doesn't mind.

"How was school, Hannah?" She takes my bag and lunch box and puts them in the back. David, my baby brother, is asleep in his car seat.

"Guess what? We had a maths test and I got the highest marks out of the whole class. And Miss Donohue gave me no homework because I did so well, and everyone else got homework."

Mum is wearing just a green T-shirt and no coat. Her hair is tied so tightly that it pulls her eyes wide open. She says, "That's good," and keeps looking straight out the windscreen. It's getting dark. Black clouds hide the sun and the rain is getting heavier. The wipers wave across the window so fast, I'm afraid they'll fly off. Inside, the glass is cloudy. With a yellow cloth, Mum wipes a circle clear.

I sit back. It will be better telling Daddy about my tests. He'll call me a little genius and maybe even buy me a treat. I look out the window. In front of us is a man on a bike. He's wearing a black rain jacket and the wind is blowing it into a big balloon. He is so close, he looks like he could be sitting on top of me.

"Mum!"

I cover my eyes. A thud on the windscreen makes me jump and I close my eyes tighter. The brakes screech and the car stops. David wakes.

"Fuck! Fuck, fuck, fuck." Mum stares ahead. Her hands are white, clenching the steering wheel. The car engine hums. I breathe into my hands. The man has landed in the ditch with his bike beside him, tangled up like a squashed number eight. He doesn't move. His round black back pokes out of the grass. It doesn't look like a person. It looks like a black sack of rubbish.

"Mum?"

"Be quiet." She rests her elbows on the steering wheel and drums her knuckles on her forehead. David whimpers in the back seat.

"It's okay, baby." She turns and picks up his teddy bear, which has fallen to the floor. She holds it for a few minutes, squeezing it in both hands, then tucks it in beside him. She looks up and down the road. It's empty. She looks again, and drives on.

"Mum?"

"Be quiet, Hannah."

A sob starts in my belly and gurgles up through my throat.

"Stop crying. There's nothing wrong with you," Mum says, without looking. I swallow my sobs.

Eight times nought is nothing.

Eight times one is eight.

Eight times two is sixteen.

Eight times three is twenty-four.

When I was little, before I learned maths tables, I recited other things: songs, nursery rhymes, or the alphabet, over and over again, until I had forgotten whatever I was thinking.

Eight times four is thirty-two.

Eight times five is forty.

Sometimes I'll go higher than the tables I learned at school, multiplying by thirteen or fourteen. Then I have to concentrate really hard to keep singing the sums and work them out in my head.

Eight times six is forty-eight.

"It was his fault. He was too far out on the road." Mum breaks my concentration. She is staring at the road ahead, gripping the wheel. Is she talking to me or to herself?

"If we tell anyone, I'll be taken away. Is that what you want?" She turns up the heat. The whooshing fan gets louder. I think about my maths test, how I got ten out of ten, and try to get back that happy feeling. But I keep seeing that man, pedalling in front of the car.

Nine times nought is nothing.

Nine times one is nine.

We pull into the drive. My pink and white bicycle is lying on the lawn. I should put it in the shed. Mum always says it will be my own fault if the bike is ruined from the rain. She says if I can't look after my things that I shouldn't have them. I hope she doesn't see the bike now.

"Don't tell anyone," she says quietly.

She turns in her seat to face me. Her skin is white and her eyes are big and shiny like marbles. Her chest goes up and down with each breath. Her hands shake.

"Everything will be okay if you don't tell anyone, Hannah. Do you understand?"

I wish this had never happened. I wish it was yesterday, even though I got in trouble for spilling David's milk. I wouldn't mind that now. I'd just have to say I'm sorry and clean up the mess. Mum reaches out and puts her hands over mine. They are hot and damp. They feel strange; smaller and smoother than Daddy's.

"Promise me. It will be our secret. Just between you and me."

I know that we should call someone, the police or an ambulance, but I push away the thought. She is holding my hand and looking right at me. It's like I'm the only person that matters. Not Daddy, not even

David. Just us. Our secret. Just between me and my mum.

"I promise," I say. "I won't tell anyone."

She gives me a half-smile.

"Good girl." That smile almost makes me forget about the man lying in the ditch beside his crushed bicycle.

We have mashed potatoes, beans and burgers for dinner. Daddy sticks a fork in his burger and holds it up.

"What's this?" he asks Mum.

"Don't eat it if you don't want it."

I eat mine. The potato slides down my throat in lumps and I swallow extra hard. Daddy eats all of his, even though it's from the freezer and not a proper after-work dinner. David gurgles happily and bangs his plastic spoon on the highchair. Mum feeds him potatoes and gravy. It's his favourite. She barely touches her own.

I have no homework, so I get ready for bed early and kiss Daddy goodnight.

"You're very quiet tonight, Hannah," he says.

I make myself smile.

"Will you read for me until I fall asleep?"

"Ahh, Hannah, you're too old for that. Go on to bed now." He kisses my forehead. "Sweet dreams."

I count the stairs. Seventeen steps to my bedroom.

The body in the grass is stuck on the back of my eyelids. When I close my eyes to sleep, I see his hand moving, reaching for the road. I turn on the light and keep my eyes open to keep him out. I concentrate on the things in my room. I study the lines in the wood of my wardrobe. I look at the books I've lined up on the shelves in the order that I read them. I multiply, I count the flowers on my wallpaper, hug my panda bear tight. The television hums downstairs and Daddy laughs. Mum laughs too.

At breakfast, Mum is just like she is every morning; putting a pot of tea in front of Daddy, mixing David's breakfast in a blue plastic bowl, wrapping my cheese sandwiches in crinkly tinfoil and packing them in my bag.

Daddy leaves for work, and tugs my hair on his way past. I forgot to tell him about my maths test.

"Bye," he calls as he picks up his briefcase and car keys in the hall. Mum takes David out of his chair.

"Get ready for school," she tells me.

"Is the man dead?" I ask.

"What man?"

Weeks pass and no one comes to take her away. I feel as if I have briars in my stomach. In school I see his daughter. She is two years older than me, in sixth class. I watch her in the yard at lunchtime and wonder who gives her bedtime hugs now. Who will look after her family and put food on the table? Surrounded by girls, she sits with her back to the wall. She catches me looking and makes a face at me. But everyone stares at her. She is the girl whose father was killed.

My best friend, Ellen, talks about her new puppy; how he buries bones under her pillow. I pretend to listen, although I can't laugh and I cannot think of anything funny to tell her.

But school is still my very favourite place. When I'm in the classroom I don't think about him at all. I think about the answers to Miss Donohue's questions. My maths gets even better. I do sums without making any mistakes and I start to learn about distance, weight and speed. Miss Donohue has to give me a new workbook. She says I'm solving problems like a demon. That's fast. So she gets me to make up my own questions and problems. I try to think of really hard ones; questions that take a long time to figure out.

On the way to bed, I step only on stairs that are prime numbers. I multiply and multiply in my head, all the way up to the fifteen times tables. But I can't keep out the dreams about the man. He crawls out of the ditch to the side of the road, stretches out his hand and gives me a key. It's raining so hard that water drips off my face and my skin is wet through my clothes. The sun is falling out of the sky and it's getting darker and darker. I use the key to lock Mum and David in the car.

She shouts at me: "You promised, Hannah. You've broken your promise."

David cries; his face all wrinkled and as red as the car.

I wake up with a scream. Daddy hears me and comes to my room. "Hannah?"

There are tears on my face. I dry them with my duvet.

"Did you have a bad dream?" He sits on the bed beside me, leaning forward, his face close to mine, and his hands on my arms. "What's upsetting you, Hannah?"

I want to ask him to make the bad dreams stop, but my mouth is full of sobs. Mum comes to the door. "What's wrong?"

"She had a bad dream."

Mum moves over to the bed and stands behind Daddy.

"What was it about?" Daddy asks me.

"There was a man on a bike," I say. "But it was raining. We couldn't see him."

Daddy hugs me. "Sshhh. It's okay. It was just a dream."

The school holidays come. David can stand up all by himself and tries to say words. He calls me Ha, but Mum says it's just baby noise. She hardly talks to me now. Maybe she thinks I told. I'm trying so hard to keep our secret, but the pictures of the man are in my head all the time. Maybe I said it out loud in my sleep. Or maybe Miss Donohue guessed because I'm working like a demon, or Daddy guessed, or Ellen, or the man's daughter. But I didn't break my promise. If they guessed, it wouldn't be my fault.

Daddy asks: "What's the matter, Hannah? You can tell me."

But I can't.

So I practice maths. I write a problem. I think about it for a long time. I think about all the numbers and how to put them in the right place. I read about speed. I measure out distances. I think about all the different answers. And I write this question: if a car is driving at fifty kilometres per hour and there is a man on a bicycle one metre in front, can the car stop before it hits the man? I write the problem, but I don't know the answer. Maybe I'll show Daddy, or Miss Donohue. Maybe they'll know what to do.

Maura Amy Roosevelt

—⊷⊶⊷—

Going South

They must have been in Georgia already. Mile-high pine trees loomed above titanium light poles. Rain was coming down at the car in a funny, sideways sheet. Misting over the windshield. The news was always saying they lived in a post-rain era, but that wasn't true. The sky still drizzled and spat at the world; it just never came down in buckets, with confidence. They were in the clunker: the Chevy Malibu that smelled of cigarettes smoked years ago and had stains from coffee spilled on the mats that was never mopped up. The car belonged to Violet's mom but they had taken it with them on this adventure.

Violet looked at the newly fragile state of her husband as he hunched over the steering wheel. He had been eating less and less and had lost so much weight recently. When she met Kurt he was one of those fumbling boys with shoulders too broad and legs too thick for the rest of his childlike physique. His head hung as he lumbered through the crowded streets surrounding Manhattan College, seeming surprised by his own largeness. He had a shock of loopy blond hair, and that – in addition to standing a good eight inches over the crowd at all times – differentiated him from the herd, and drew a person's eyes upward to him, the sky-scrapers, the clouds, and the afternoon sun that rippled above his head. From the first moment Violet saw Kurt standing on the corner of

Mercer and East 4th Street handing out flyers for an Antediluvialist rally, she was literally looking up to him.

Kurt hadn't driven since he got accepted to college and declared himself a New Yorker. Now double-barrelled oil trucks sped by them at ninety miles an hour while their Chevy was ticking along at fifty-five. He was breathing deeply, his eyes fixed through the windshield. The rain was beginning to separate into drops but the sun still shone through them. It was nothing the two of them hadn't seen before, this type of rain. Kurt turned the chugging vehicle into a highway gas station and pulled it halfway into a spot on the edge of the pavement. He cut the engine and swung open his door, pitching his body out through the air until he hit the browned grass, smiling and shrieking. He rolled all the way down the burnt grass parking lot hill.

"We're alive!" he yelled through the well-spaced raindrops. "I didn't kill us in the car; we're alive!" The goofball. "We made it!"

He jumped to his feet and bounded over to Violet, who was shoeless now, leaning against the passenger side of the car, puffing her black bangs and rolling her eyes. He grabbed her and attempted to pick her up and press her whole body against the car, wrapping her two legs around him. But he couldn't do it. He struggled for nearly a minute before his arms went limp and he headed to the gas pump.

When he was finished filling up the tank, Kurt wandered down the hill to take a piss in a thicket of sycamore and birch trees. Minutes later he called up to Violet: "Vi, you gotta see this!" Kurt was zipping up his fly when she found him, and they walked together to the other side of the trees. A space the size of a football field opened up before them. In the field there was an oblong abandoned building, divided into various numbered rooms and covered in grey and rotting shingles. Most of the front doors were off their hinges or missing entirely.

"What do you think this place is?" Violet asked, while leading the way down the line of empty rooms.

"It was a motel, once upon a time," Kurt answered, surveying the site.

"But can you imagine it being full of customers? Way out here in the middle of nowhere, just burned up fields and highways on both sides."

At the end of the row of rooms stood a partially demolished stand-alone house. It was as if someone had dropped a giant sledgehammer on it, making half of it crumble down to the dirt. Wood and bricks and nails and insulation had been blasted every-which-way and then forgotten about.

The two of them crawled inside the collapsed house frame. Kurt kicked straight through the rubble and picked up what looked like a concrete block, but was actually made of Styrofoam. He threw it out of the house-shell with ease, smiling like a bad child.

"What's on your mind there, Kurtis Harte?" Violet asked.

"We should move here! We should move here, Vi."

He had found his way to a doorframe with no walls or ceilings above it, and was lifting himself up on it, his thin arms pumping through pull-ups.

She smiled at him. He was still a beautiful man. "There was a 'For Sale' sign back there in the middle of the corn field. I'll bet this is what's selling."

"Imagine it! Just imagine it. We could get all our friends out here, and everyone would have their own little room," Kurt said.

Violet was nodding and climbing through the rubble in her bare feet. The rain had stopped since they got out of the car and the sun was out in full again. Through the sparse tree branches they could see that the traffic on the other side of the highway had stopped. Although there were people in the backed-up cars, there wasn't a sound to be heard. It was perfectly quiet. Those Georgia rays were out for sure then, spanking down on Violet's bare shoulders and the bridge of her nose.

"This is how everyone was meant to live. There's so much space out here, everyone would be at peace. We could grow things. We'd want to work together," Kurt said, locking his gaze into hers. He put his arms around her waist and was able to pick her up just for a second until she put her toes on the tops of his sneakers.

"Me and you, we could rebuild this house. We could build it back up, all ramshackle, and build a bedroom for us and a kitchen that everyone would use. You and me in the big house."

She kissed him and it smelled like sweat, both stale and new. The white clouds started to part above them. Violet investigated the sky and noticed black clouds to the east, rising upward like some kind of second coming from the dark side. They were far off in the distance, but black like she'd never seen.

"We should get going, maybe," she whispered.

Kurt looked up at the sky, perplexed. "I guess it's gonna rain again."

And sure enough, the raindrops started. Though it was warm outside, these drops were falling with urgency: they weren't big, take-your-time, juicy raindrops. They fell like bullets from the sky.

The young couple stomped through the thicket back to the car. Violet took the driver's seat this time; she was more comfortable with it. As they pulled away from the rubble motel, she glimpsed a hole in the tree growth, in her rear-view mirror. She could see a corner of the half-destroyed house and behind it a dock leading out into a river they hadn't noticed before. As she pulled the car into reverse, she could see that the dock was broken, and most of its right side was submerged in water. She imagined herself and Kurt sitting at the end of the waterlogged pier at the bottom of a sunny afternoon. The night would be rising around them, buzzing with fireflies. There would be a heaviness in the air and their legs would dangle off the edge like Spanish moss. The two of them would sit there on the dock in silence with the sun falling above, and the river would have flecks of shimmering gold swimming through it.

Violet drove through the rain and thought about how things could get better. Maybe they really would move down here, away from the North and all that came with it. Recently she and the other Antediluvialists in New York spent the majority of their days recycling the bottles they had drunk at whatever party they'd been to the night before. To Antediluvialists, Southerners were the last remaining remnants of the olden days, when everything was right and natural. Southerners were people of the earth, the brine of the past, the roux for a new beginning.

Kurt was already in charge of the college chapter of the Antediluvialists when she'd met him. Of course, there was technically no leader, and the doctrines forbade having an authority figure in charge. But then there was Kurt. It was artless and easy; people wanted to listen to him.

Violet had opened the door to her first meeting in the attic room of Judson Church just as the incantation was being repeated. "*We believe in a time before the flood. We believe in the natural order of the agrarian world. We believe the flood will come again, and nature shall be returned to right and earthly order.*"

Kurt was addicted to The Cause. Soon enough Violet was too. After a mere few weeks of meetings she began to realise: she had always been an Antediluvialist. She was anti-modernity, morally opposed to a society that belonged to *them* and not *her*. She had always just thought she was cynical, yet she had never known why before. Oh to find herself!

She married Kurt just over a year before they decided to take this trip, right after he'd graduated from college. Antediluvialists preach the uselessness and petty bourgeois reasonableness of higher education, and so she had dropped out when Kurt graduated. Violet's mother had cried while Kurt's mother framed the certificate he got from the President of the University which said his GPA was among the highest in school history. On the night of his graduation Kurt had treated Violet to a candle-lit dinner on the rooftop of their collective house. Stars hung low over the Brooklyn Bridge, twinkling above the cursive graffiti on the tops of buildings. The graffiti read: *You Go Girl!* And: *I Still Love You.* Kurt told her he was proud of her for "doing what she did and getting free." She called him a cheese-puff. A sweet-corny fritter. It was a beautiful night.

Now Violet knew all of the spoken and unspoken tenets of the movement. The way to be the perfect Antediluvialist wife is to learn to share. Have your own bed in his house and when a new girl is travelling through: "Hello, my name is Rose," let her sleep in his bed and you go to yours, and never admit that it bothers you. You are cooler than that. Stay composed. You are a woman, and you want to do extraordinary things. Like keep this guy. Two weeks later Lily comes to town and you're on your own again, and you can hear them through the wall, pounding. You put a pillow over your head and think about Antediluvialism. No body is nobody's private property. Lily giggles and whispers to him, "Are you close?" And you hear it. You cry in front of him and he tells you that your face looks bloated when you're sad. He thought you were cooler than that.

While making good time on I-75, Violet finally heard an earnest man's voice speaking clearly out of the car radio. "Severe storm warning," the voice reported as Kurt dozed evenly beside her. "From Western Mississippi to Northern Georgia, tropical storms threaten the region. Stay tuned for more in-depth reporting on this emerging weather."

Tropical storms? They had planned on camping out in a place called Tallulah Gorge. A tent and pegs and one sleeping bag were all in the trunk, courtesy of Violet's parents' basement. She punched Kurt in the shoulder to wake him, and he opened his eyes in mock anger.

"WOMAN!" he blundered. "What did I tell you about wakin' me?" He was still in his high-spirited mood.

"Supposedly this storm is going to keep coming. I think it's going to screw up our camping plans. Maybe even slow us down. You think we'll get to Georgia in time to go swimming?"

"Ain't no little storm gonna slow us down, baby."

"I think it's a big storm. We've never seen anything like a tropical storm, Kurt."

The rain was more than steady: it came down in blankets, making it hard to see the road. The double-barrelled trucks were wavering in and out of the lane beside the Chevy. Their car pointed south while the lanes going north on I-75 began to fill so full of cars that traffic was slowing to a stop again.

Kurt was wide awake and playing with the radio dial now. He settled on a barely audible woman's voice. "Hurricane," the voice was saying. That was one of two words they could make out. The other was:

"Evacuate."

It was four in the afternoon but most of the light had gone out of the sky.

"I think I want to stay in a regular hotel tonight," Violet told Kurt.

"We can't do that," Kurt said. "We're adventurers! Antediluvialists! If it wasn't raining, I'd make you sleep next to me right on the shoulder of the road over there. And I'd make you do it naked!"

"Now you're a comedian. Seriously. We need to be inside. I don't think that what's happening outside is just a little storm."

"I'm not staying in a damn hotel. I don't do stuff like that. But you can have a great time on your own."

"Come on. I'm not going anywhere without you. I'll pay for it. I'll pay for the whole thing," Violet said.

"What are you, a bourgeois asshole?"

"I just want to be safe, is all."

"What, you believe the things they say now?"

They were silent for the next hour and a half that it took them to get to Tallulah Gorge.

Violet found signs pointing off the highway to the campground. The car grumbled over the stones in the dirt road, making its way down the hill. The rain was falling fast and the wheels skidded twice; the road was turning to mud. Down at the base of the hill was a wooden house with striated white paint peeling off of it. *Main Office* was spray painted over a screen door. She parked the car beside it.

"Should we really be camping now, Kurt? It's worse out there than it has been in years."

Kurt uttered "c'mon," under his breath, and slammed the passenger's side door.

The inside of the office smelled damp and mouldy and there was a draught running through it. A guy was perched behind the counter. He had long stringy brown hair and teeth that were matching in colour. The front right one was missing. He looked at them sidelong.

"Well, by God. I didn't think there'd be anybody coming in to see me today."

"Oh we're here to see you alright," Kurt answered. "You got campsites available?"

Kurt's voice had acquired a twang since they had left New York. Violet didn't think it was on purpose – just an involuntary tick. But the man still guffawed.

"Northerners! Well I never. Northerners, here on the rainiest of Sundees. Y'all even know how to camp? They even teach you how to feed yourself up there?"

Violet smiled. "Sure thing, hon. We know how to do all of that." Might as well join in on the accent, since Kurt had got it started.

The guy whistled through the space in his teeth. "Jesus, you sure got the purdiest wife I ever seen," he said to Kurt, while looking Violet up and down.

"She sure is, idn't she," Kurt replied.

The man chuckled. "Well alright, kids. I recommend you take the best campsite we got going for us, seeing as there's nobody else around here today. An' I tell ya what, I'm gonna give y'all a discount. Just hold on a second there an' I'll git my clipboard."

He turned and disappeared through a doorway that led to a back room, revealing a poster hanging on the wood-panelled wall behind him. It was three feet by four feet, glossy and curling at the edges. The picture on the poster was of a tiny skeletal body: it had a miniature arm, a leg, and an open rib cage. All were coated in a mucous-sheen layer of blood and gore. A foetus. There was the bulbous shape of a miniature head lolling forward, with unformed covered eyes and more carnage clotted at the base of it. At the bottom of it white block letters spelled out: AN EYE FOR AN EYE.

Violet examined the sign and nausea rang up inside her. She turned and scrambled outside, letting the screen door snap before vomiting onto the wet mulch. Kurt followed her out. Now their clothes were soaking.

She coughed and wiped her mouth. "Get in the car, Kurt! We're leaving."

"I don't want to leave. What's your problem?"

She was dizzy but she went straight to the driver's seat. Exasperated, Kurt went to the passenger seat and closed the door with a wham.

"What is my problem?" Violet hollered. "Did you not see that picture? My problem? I'm not going to give a cent to someone like that."

They were halfway back to the motel they had passed at the highway exit, Butch's Roadside Inn, when Kurt replied. "You are a goddamn product of where you come from."

Inside their room at Butch's the television showed footage of New Orleans under water. Levees had broken and the streets and cars were submerged. People were riding through neighbourhoods on motorboats. Water had engulfed houses up to their second storey windows and whole families were screaming at the news helicopters from their roofs. Infants in diapers, grandmothers in robes; everyone was crying. Kurt and Violet sat on the synthetic bedspread and watched the horrific images without a word. Newscasters were tallying up projected deaths and turning to one another, asking: "How could this happen?"

Outside their motel room rain was coming down artillery fire, pelting the ground and bouncing back up with force. Sycamore trees were swaying in unreal movements, trunks bending at the waist, leaves and branches sweeping the ground, grasping. A limb broke off at the shoulder and crashed against the highway pavement.

The boom of the crash made Kurt get up and push the door open. He walked outside and stood on the green grass of the road bank. He put his arms up to the sky, and then his face. Violet went to the open doorway and watched him. He looked like a reed being blown back and forth, thin, with intermittent hair clumping upwards. There was a sound, like a bird squawking rhythmically, mechanically. It took her a moment to realise it was coming from Kurt. Laughter? And then he lowered his head and faced her: he was sobbing, although there was a fixed tension in his face. A smile. Rain ran over his face and down his cheeks, and his tears mixed into it. He swung his arms around his body in a circle.

"The flood," he yelled to her. "The flood! It's here." His squawking sob was interrupted by victory yells now. "The time is now, Violet. I'm going further south – this is it! The revolution will begin! The flood came back. I've got to go south and claim it."

He ran to where she was standing in the doorway and put his arms on her shoulders. "Are you coming with me? Are you going to follow me down?"

He dipped his head backward into the stream of water coming off the eave of the inn. It poured over his face and he smiled, drinking some of it in and shaking his head like a dog.

Violet articulated slowly: "You cannot go anywhere, Kurt. There's nowhere to go. You will die."

She watched her words reach Kurt and boomerang back to her without being heard. He looked peculiar; this was not the same person she had met on Mercer and East 4th Street. Kurt laughed and dropped his arms, stepping back into the rain.

"I'm going," he shouted. "I'm going right now!"

He took another step backward into the parking lot and looked up at the shadowy sky and then across the four lanes of empty roadway to a billboard swaying back and forth.

"I did this!" He screamed a rebel yell. His right hand beat his chest violently and then shot into the air. "I did all this." He laughed with his whole body and looked at Violet with yellow eyes, before turning and running down the highway.

She could only see him for a minute or two, a fuzzy grey figure moving away from the motel at a rabbit's pace. The last thing she heard from him, through the whirring and clattering noise all around her was his fervent, guttural cry: "I made it rain!"

Annemarie Ní Churreáin

Lifeline

Pregnant. The new fact is a tendril
taking hold of every word, curling
in on breaths the way commas do,
half-lit and prim as cuticle-moons.

Between us, empty goblets reflect
clear amazement: what will happen
to childless escapades past midnight
into the company of small, light hours

or to late sleeping through mornings,
whilst in the hallway, dogs circle cats,
all tails lifting to the sound of mail
being whispered underneath a door?

Some part of me does not want this
change to our friendship, although –
I should by now trust in your ability
to mother change in uncertain places,

just as you began in South America,
despite strange rains, to nurture this
newness in your womb that you say
flutters like a kiss across your skin.

A kiss. I lay down in a bath until
the surface floats up below my chin
and my own menses blood casts a
lifeline out through the water.

The Parting

When he was a young man
making love to college girls
in civil darkness,

she was a child still,
crossing borders
in the North of Ireland,

being blinded by soldiers,
with pictures pressed like receipts
into their wallets,

who bore torch-lights
through car windows
at people wanting only home.

Guns over shoulders
glowed bright as silver prey
pulled from foothold traps.

This was her life:
travelling through unrest
into safer territories,

until placing a hand
on his face, she knew –
there was no safety in this

and under no rained confetti,
no proud shells,
no ceremony,

they parted lives in a church
where birds circled passively,
in high, blue lofts

and their own voices,
echoed in hallways,
were thin as wires

transmitting
long, silk gloves of moonlight
into starless endings.

House

On that grave, bare soil I could return completely,
feel my way back towards the centre as a blind woman might,
with only love as her guide.

In the wide open where not a single thing grows now,
the one sure thing is memory:
rooms, nooks, all the cherished holding-places survive.

The stacked delph, the black trunk brought from America by ship,
the box of photographs beneath the table in the high bedroom.
I could reach through darkness, find them every time

and know immediately – the earth underfoot, where in summer
we set out chairs to watch who was coming in,
going out at Kit Dhonnachaidh's hill.

Fantasies

Me: in an apron with front pockets
and a pussy-bow in my hair,

making sponge cakes
that spring up beneath a finger's tip

and remain on the sideboard,
uneaten and unpicked at

until thick slices served out
make no one who visits ill.

You: making a table
and plenty of noise in the garden shed,

measuring up planks
behind locked, oak doors,

making things right,
putting all sorts together,

whenever anyone knocks,
you sound busy and handsome.

In the middle of the night
you rise without complaint

to fetch me a glass of water,
not because I have asked

but because you feel
the pattern of my breathing has changed

from low to lowish-shallow
and that I might need a drink before dawn.

We Can Plant a Mango Tree in the Back Yard

Lifted snow reveals a city glistening
in new, thin skins of attic light.
We button up our winter coats,
turn collars out against the wind.

Along the bright canal, we speed
past swans in gentle, necklace sleep.
From the end of her cigarette,
signals rise unread into the cool air.

There are coffees, tall drinks, seats
pushed together in corners: every hour
I spend with her is a crossed border,
a new claim on land, a strange tongue.

Beneath the light weight of cotton,
her breathing keeps me awake for hours,
my heart beats against her middle back,
dreams at her spine's curve.

"Please" and "do" I whisper invisibly.
Our birth-year is the same. I can live
with your hidden marks. We can
plant a mango tree in the back yard.

Like an island, her dark head floats
across a white ocean to my pillow
and my hand on her face feels Asia
radiating warmth through my bones.

In the morning, before she leaves me
drifting in and out of an orchid scent,
I wake to pin a jewel on her shirt lapel
and ask for nothing more than this.

Laundry

Here in the Indian foothills,
I share a house with a man from Greece

who speaks no English perfectly,
disappears for days on a motorbike,

leaves his laundry on the low make-shift linc
grieving an absent sun.

Side by side they hang: his shirt, my summer dress
as if they know each other well

and when he returns smelling of engine oil,
monsoon, rolled brown cigarettes,

we have no formal language,
to share our separate joy.

Drip-drip on the balcony,
a queer, white pool gathers below.

He holds at a sleeve, looks to sky,
I open my palm for signs of rain.

Our Oath

By right, I should have it out with you,
put straight wrongs, draw a sword
through this silence

and maybe that's what I'd do,
if you weren't so beautiful
and not an autumn to my one falling leaf

but I can hardly breathe around you,
something in my throat closes
and it is all I can do to live

through oceanic moments
that come in, go out between us
according to the delicate hour.

Salts taste, sands disturb,
singular memories transfigure
any given rock

and drive sharp metal through me
like a hook into the mouth
of a wandered fish,

or a pill burning
on a child's tongue:
innocence and virulence meet

as once we did,
incurving on each other
with only a fool's knowledge of the consequences.

Do not mistake my wordlessness for peace:
never think that a mouth gasping
is code for no hurt

or that to part
means an end to this narrative
in which all plots lead to the same shame.

Nothing since can begin
until we first
unswear our oath.

Eva Sandoval

Elegant Tuesday

It was a cold, wet Tuesday in September, a few days after Mr. Palmer's death, when Elliott came to work wearing a tuxedo. It was such a surprise; the lovely kind, unlike the previous week's horror. Apart from Mr. Palmer, everyone always came to the office in Business Casual. No one had known what to wear to work since it happened, nor had they known what to do. For years, they'd worn sports jackets and pitched gift wrap designs; now they wore dark shirts and avoided each others' eyes. Watch hands ticked. Fingers stabbed computer keys. Lights sizzled in the ceiling. And yet, here was Elliott in black and white formal dress.

Terry was sitting at the front desk, ignoring the shrilling phones, when Elliott burst through the elevator doors, regal as a zebra.

"Well, look at you," she said, her voice cracking from days of disuse. "You're *so* very elegant. What's the occasion?"

"Oh, just trying something new," said Elliott, also hoarsely.

Jackson was slumping in the dark mail room when Elliott ducked in to collect a package. The light streaming in from the cracked door glinted off Elliott's metal shirt studs.

"Ah, Mr. Bond," said Jackson. "You've come to pick up your cufflink laser beams at last."

"Well, it *is* Tuesday," Elliott replied, signing his name on the pad with a flourish.

No one had thought to light up the office kitchen, so he snapped the switch. The fluorescent lights stuttered and bathed that day's pastry basket in a cold glow. Elliott poured himself some tea instead of coffee and took a shortbread cookie instead of a bagel. He balanced his breakfast on his package, which was flat, and carried it to his desk. To his delight, the women were already waiting for him.

"So it's true!" they cried. "We didn't believe Terry. Aren't you hand-some! Are you a spy? Eloping at lunch? Oh, just tell us why you're looking so glamorous already!"

Elliott blushed deeply, as he had at both Terry's and Jackson's comments.

"I have to go to a black tie wedding after work today," he admitted. "I came to work like this because I won't have enough time to change before I meet my sisters at the hotel."

"Ah!" smirked Sonja from Sales, drumming her fingers on her biceps. "So we have a wedding to blame for this display of male vanity. Silly me; I was sure it was an early midlife crisis. Oh, well."

"Oh, well," said Elliott.

"I have my mink in the car if you get chilly," announced Violet from Creative. "...daa-hling!"

And for the first time since Mr. Palmer had died, everybody laughed.

The next day, of course, Elliott came to work in Mourning Casual – dark slacks and a grey shirt. Terry's face lifted and fell as he passed through the silent lobby. His black shoes scraped along the carpet. Marvin from Creative crunched empty shipment boxes. The copier wheezed.

"No tuxedo today?" asked Antoinette from Accounting as Elliott passed her in the hallway.

"No, no, not today," he replied, his cheeks flaming pink. "No more weddings for a while."

"That's too bad."

"Well, I don't know," said Elliott. Her attention had made him feel bold, and his next few thoughts tumbled forth in a rush. "It wasn't that much fun. How do they expect you to enjoy your steak if you're afraid of ruining your shirt?"

"Wear a bib, silly," said Antoinette.

"And spoil the look?"

"Bah," said Antoinette. "So no more glamour. We expected more from you, Jeeves! You've set a certain standard, you know."

"I know, I know," Elliott said.

On his way back to his desk, he passed Mr. Palmer's office. The blinds were drawn shut as they'd been ever since the death, so Elliott couldn't see inside, but he thought of the tall ficus in the corner – the staff's gift to him on his last birthday.

"Gang," Mr. Palmer had once said, "If the ficus droops, I droop."

Elliott wondered if anyone had thought to water it since the man had passed away.

Sonja happened to be walking by the office at the same moment. Instead of averting their eyes in this sad stretch of hallway, she and Elliott could look each other in the face.

"Oh, Elliott," she said. "No more tuxedo? Dropping the ball, dropping the ball."

"I know."

"I have to tell you. It's just been so awful ever since Mr. Palmer..." Sonja's eyes glittered. She took a breath and peered up at the fluorescent lights burning in the panelled ceiling.

"Anyway," she said, "seeing you in that monkey suit yesterday really made things a little... brighter."

Elliott cut his eyes away, too. "Well, maybe Violet brought up that mink after all."

"Ha!" said Sonja. "Wouldn't that be something?"

The next few days crackled with black tension. They were heading into the holiday rush; Creative should have been cranking out Christmas card designs but Violet couldn't seem to make her Santas jolly enough.

The five members of the Board were barricaded inside the Conference Room as they'd been since the death, their voices rising and falling in ghostly hums. Rumours crept through the staff: Palmer Paperie would shut down; Palmer Paperie would move headquarters to Miami; Palmer Paperie would continue to run with a new Creative Director hired from the outside.

"Wrong," said Pete from Sales, grimacing at his black tie. "They're going to institute Mrs. Palmer. It's what Mr. Palmer would have wanted."

"But she's just a goddamned lawyer," snarled Sonja. "What does she know about art? What does she know about *anything* besides lying? Go away, go away. You don't know what you're talking about."

On Wednesday, the Board sent the staff their latest sympathy basket – this one spilling over with tropical fruits. On Thursday, it was consolation coffee cake. Friday, lasagna with love. On Monday, the staff was greeted by a pair of beautiful orchids flanking Terry's desk, arching towards her in a lavish purple spray. Creative, Sales, and Accounting walked through the peace plants without a word and took their seats. They craned their necks towards the hums in the Conference Room and frowned. They skimmed job ads. They ignored the food.

And then, on Tuesday, Sonja sailed into work with a cocky stride in her step; she was wearing a tight red dress. Jackson let out a shrill whistle as she sashayed past the mailroom. Elliott and Pete looked up from their reports.

"Well, well!" said Pete. "Look what we have here!"

Sonja flashed him a grin. "This li'l ol' thang?" she said, affecting a honeyed Southern drawl. "Rags, sugar. Nothin' but rags."

"Not bad," said Pete. "Get a load of her, Elliott."

Elliott looked. He noticed that Sonja's lips were coloured red to match her dress and that her black hair had been straightened. Suddenly, he felt invisible in his grey shirt – passed over, like a one-eyed puppy at the pound.

"You look nice," he said quietly.

Sonja winked and kicked up her heels; black and spiked.

"Oh, you!" cried Violet, rolling her chair over to Sales. "I honestly did think about wearing something fancy today! In honour of Elliott's tuxedo last week."

Pete corrected her: "Bond. Elliott Bond."

Elliott blushed with gratitude.

"That was fun, wasn't it?" said Sonja. "Maybe Elliott and I have started a trend!"

And that was the official start of Elegant Tuesday.

The concept evolved rapidly, with ideas exploding forth from the Elegant Tuesday Braintrust, headed by Sonja. The Official Rules landed in their inboxes on a Normal Thursday, during another Board Meeting.

> Attn: All Palmer Paperie Staff
> *The Official Elegant Tuesday Rules*:
> - The fancier the dress, the better.
> - Elegance from any era is welcome.
> - Fancy clothes must stay on all day.
> - NO rubber, denim, or elastic.
> - 1:00 p.m. is MANDATORY tea-time in the break room.
> - Clean up after yourself in the kitchen; we are ladies and gentlemen.

Normal Thursday was electrified, despite the angry gavel thumps that echoed from the conference room. On Casual Friday, Marvin helped himself to two pieces of platitude pizza, dribbling a blob of sauce on his black Queen T-shirt.

"Pig!" snorted Sonja. She hesitated slightly before also taking a slice.

The coffee dripped in the pot. The elevator doors pinged. And on Tuesday, the entire staff came to work in flurries of swishing silk and glimmering sequins. Elliott wore his tuxedo again, blushing when Jackson greeted him with a booming "Mr. Bond!" Jackson himself had come in a red velvet smoking jacket.

"You have entered my lair, Mr. Bond," he sneered when Elliott passed the mail room. "Prepare to..." He caught himself short. Both men grimaced.

"Yoo hoo!" cried Violet, gliding between them. "Hello, gentlemen. Don't you look sharp!"

Jackson and Elliott regarded her appreciatively; she was stunning herself in a pink satin gown layered with flashing costume jewellery.

"How about you!" said Jackson. "You're like Grace Kelly at the Oscars."

"Why, thank you, Mr. Hefner!" said Violet.

"Come by the mail room later," said Jackson. "I've got a package for you."

"Oh, Jackson!" Violet swished away, leaving a trail of giggles behind her.

Elliott aimed a laser beam cufflink at Jackson before heading back to Sales, where Pete was showing off the powder blue tuxedo from his wedding in 1982.

"Look," he said, fluffing his ruffled shirt to emphasise his tight waistline. "It still fits!"

Antoinette rushed between desks, her legs rustling in her full taffeta skirt. "Did everyone see?" she asked. "The Board ordered scones for us today!"

Eight pairs of gleaming dress shoes tramped into the bright kitchen and beheld baskets heaping with strawberry-studded pastry.

"Finally, something decent," said Sonja.

"Isn't it *divine*?" asked Violet. "Now who'd like some tea?"

"I would," said Elliott from behind the crowd.

"Oh, Jeeves!" said Violet. "Of course you would!"

"I'll pour."

"I'll drink!"

"Will you have tea?" Sonja asked Marvin.

"Only if it comes with a shot of scotch," he said.

The hot water hissed. The tea bags plopped into the Styrofoam cups. And everybody laughed.

It was a different kind of elegance. They had, of course, seen each other in black suits and pearls at Mr. Palmer's funeral. The formality of that occasion had embarrassed them, especially to see Mrs. Palmer and their children huddled around the casket. They had seen the children in the office from time to time, dropped off by a nanny after school. Two little girls, both blonde and robust, streaking through the halls to show Terry the cartoons their father had drawn for them. To see them weeping had been unbearable. They were so very young. And Mr. Palmer's death had been so unexpected after all.

The first Elegant Tuesday passed and then the second. Sonja wore a low-cut emerald green number, Pete wore an ascot and, to all appearances, both the company and the new office custom were still standing. Mourning Casual attire, job searches, and cordiality still went for the Normal days of the week, but Elegant Tuesdays were just fabulous.

On Elegant Tuesday IV, Sonja amended the rules to include Fifteen-Minute Dance Parties; held during tea times. Pete was the one who knew how to hook up an mp3 player to a computer, so he became the Master of Ceremonies. The Master of Ceremonies favoured Big Band and Disco. Whatever the soundtrack, Sonja always asked Marvin to waltz, although neither of them really could. Her curls bobbed as their fake waltz turned into a fake tango. Everyone knew about Sonja and Marvin; they had been the office gossip for a full week after the previous year's Christmas Party. It had been a wonderful evening. Mr. Palmer had rented a karaoke machine, sprung for a Turducken, and designed the Winter Wonderland holiday decorations himself: glittering fir trees, origami snowflakes, and giant snowmen cut-outs not offered in their Holiday Catalogue.

Drunk, Sonja had clung to him.

"You're so cool, Mr. Brandon Palmer," she had said. "So cool." Then she had spilled her rum punch, the red splash bleeding into her tight white sweater. She had begun to cry. After Mr. Palmer patted her back soothingly, Marvin steered her to the ladies' room. It was Violet who saw them kissing behind a tissue paper poinsettia and Antoinette who spotted them climbing into a cab. But Sonja and Marvin remained bafflingly casual at work and, as far as anyone knew, their tryst had only been a one-night stand. Seeing them dressed elegantly and waltzing in the break room somehow lent a trace of dignity to their affair; everybody clapped as best as they could while holding onto a full tea cup.

"Oh, daa-hlings," said Violet at 1:15. "We *must* do this again next week."

Through her long false lashes, Antoinette smiled at still-slim Pete, who smiled at breathless Sonja, who smiled at tuxedo-ed Elliott. It was so nice to see each other this way; clapping white-gloved hands and adjusting Windsor-knotted ties. Graceful. Smiling. Despite the silliness of it all.

It was Elegant Tuesday X when Violet bumped into Mr. Stone in the hallway. Mr. Stone was one of the Board members. He was the one with the thumping gavel. As he passed Violet, he tossed an irritated snort in her direction. Violet was wrapped in her mink. A tiara nested atop her beehive.

"Still with the dress up?" asked Mr. Stone. "Maybe we should start selling masquerade invites."

Violet went to the kitchen. Elliott was already there, buttering blueberry scones for the Sales department. She told him what Mr. Stone had said.

"What do you think he meant?" she asked.

"It sounds positive to me," he said. "We can't sell anything if we're defunct."

"That's what I thought, too," she said. "I'll take my leave of thee now, Sir Elliott. I'm going to tell Lady Sonja."

Elliott's butter knife clattered in the sink. Pete's high-heeled disco shoes scraped the floor. Benny Goodman's orchestra sent an ominous tattoo through the halls. And the next week, a memo. It was finally decided: Palmer Paperie would continue to run. The search for a new Creative Director was underway. Soon, a parade of applicants trampled through the lobby; kids right out of art school for the most part and ill-at-ease in their suits.

"Look at them," read Pete's e-mail to Elliott. "Fresh-faced little farts. They make me sick."

"Me, too," typed Elliott. "But at least we still have jobs."

"I guess," Pete replied.

Three applicants came through on Elegant Tuesday XI, whispering their names to Terry and attempting to appear sensitive to the company's loss when shaking hands with the Board Chair. Sonja was debuting a blue 1940s pin up dress that day; hourglass-shaped and paired with black seamed stockings. Marvin had rented a tuxedo with tails for his weekly waltz. Violet felt a sadistic satisfaction when one of the applicants started in surprise to see her reading her e-mail through a monocle.

It was a Normal Thursday when the Board called the meeting in the conference room. A tall, middle-aged man in a grey suit stood next to them. He had a rabbit-like little face. Silver strands glittered throughout his ponytail.

"Okay, everyone," said Mr. Gill. "I'd like to introduce you all to Vincent Long. He will be our new Creative Director here at... the office. Mr. Long, would you like to say a few words?"

"Sure, Brian," said the man. "Hi, everyone. As Mr. Gill said, I'm Vincent. I'm originally from Georgia and moved here to Tampa Bay just a few months ago. I'm trying to get into the Bucs but my heart still roots for the Bulldogs. Ha ha."

Nobody laughed.

"Anyway," said Mr. Long. "I have to say that I'm impressed by the way this staff plays together. The day I came in for my interview, you were all dressed up beautifully. Were you headed somewhere together after work?"

Antoinette cleared her throat loudly. Sonja gripped her biceps.

"It's something the staff has been doing," said Mr. Gill. "Kind of a reversal of Casual Friday."

"Well, I like it," said Mr. Long. "I've been looking for an excuse to dust off my tuxedo."

The next Elegant Tuesday, Elliott wore ragged jeans and a stained yellow T-shirt. His hair clung to his skull in grimy strands and his face pulsed with stubble. There was a cold glint in his eye which made Violet draw her mink tighter around her and embarrassed Marvin while he was nursing his pipe.

"Well," said Elliott, when Terry asked. "It's not like I have money to dry clean my tuxedo every week. I work for a living."

Elliott passed the mailroom, where Jackson adjusted the buttons of his tan Mao suit jacket. The light from the cracked door glinted off Elliott's beard stubble.

"Ah. Mr... Horton," said Jackson. "I wasn't expecting you."

Elliott went into the kitchen. He snatched a bagel off of the tray and crammed it into his mouth, letting crumbs spray onto the counter.

"What the hell, Elliott," groused Sonja when he passed her desk. "You look like a hobo."

By the next Tuesday, everyone except Sonja was wearing their regular clothes again.

"Guys," said Sonja as first Marvin and then Violet trooped into the office wearing slacks and button-downs. "Guys. What the hell. Come on."

At 1:15, Sonja pulled Pete's arm. "The music. Crank it."

"Enough," said Pete. "I'm doing budgets."

Sonja turned to Elliott. His sneakers were up on his desk and a napkin was tucked into his shirt.

"Elliott," she said. "Let's dance."

Elliott looked at her. Her mascara had formed black smudges under her eyes and her lipstick had seeped into the feathery lines around her pursed mouth.

"I don't dance," he said.

Sonja's features split with rage.

"Thanks for nothing," she said.

At 2:00 Mr. Long arrived for the day, rustling through the orchids framing Terry's desk. He was wearing a white tuxedo. Green studs gleamed in his shirt. As he surveyed the plain clothed staff, a red stain crept up past his collar.

"Hi," he said at last. "I thought we were dressing up today. Looks like it's just you and me, uh –" he searched Sonja's face, then her flapper dress. "I'm sorry. I don't know your name."

Sonja's eyes shimmered. When Mr. Long turned the corner, she lifted a Post-It off her desk and kissed it until her lipstick was rubbed off. It left behind a bloody red stain.

The next Tuesday, Sonja arrived in khaki pants and a blue blouse. The tea bags in the kitchen went untouched. There was no waltz. Violet didn't call anyone "daa-hling." Elliott was no longer Mr. Bond.

And that was the end of Elegant Tuesday.

In all honesty, Elliott was relieved. It had angered him when Sonja came to work that first Tuesday in that little red dress. She wasn't just mocking him – she had stolen his attention and he had hated her for it. But that was Sonja for you. As long as he'd worked with her, she had always been that way. He had to let it go.

He would come to work from now on in the kind of clothes he'd always worn before the music, the tiaras, and the scones. Light beige suits. Loafers. Button-down shirts. The shirts might have a pocket for his pens. They might have starched collars. They might also have French cuffs, fit for a pair of magnificent metal cufflinks. Just in case.

Sara Baume

The Most Extraordinary
Sound in All the World

A dead sperm whale has exploded while being delivered to a research centre near the south-western city of Tainan. Passers-by and cars were soaked in blood, and body parts were sprayed over a road after the bursting of the whale, which was being carried on a trailer. The whale had died earlier on a beach and had been collected so that its remains could be used for educational purposes. A marine biologist blamed the explosion on pressure from gases building up in the mammal as it began to decompose.

BBC News (29-01-04)

Amid the rock-pools, archways, ledges, platforms, stacks, stumps, caves, coves, crags and crevasses that pock the ravaged surface of the west coast, there is a starfish re-growing its severed tentacles, a beefy beadlet-anemone attempting to stun a baby sprat, a hermit-crab trying on an aluminium bottle cap to shield its squashy abdomen, a puffin shedding its coloured beak, a million barnacles wriggling imperceptibly within their clustered calcifications. Beyond the toothed edges of the cliff face and toward the tumbling depths of the North Atlantic Ocean, there is a pollock glinting brown and bronze about the submerged wreckage of a fishing boat, two species of cold water coral weaving a reef out of worm tubes, a raft of phytoplankton photosynthesising in the sunlight, and a pod of long-finned pilot whales migrating southwards in pursuit of squid, their stubbed beaks and bulged foreheads ploughing neatly through the offshore waves.

Unlike the prancing porpoises and torpedoing seals, the whales are characteristically un-acrobatic. They lumber through the ripples, favouring stealth and consistency over speed and ostentation. Yet still there is one member of the herd that can no longer take the pace. The eldest bull, almost sixty years of age, flags and falls behind. He holds back and watches as the paddling tail-flukes of his fellows shrink into the murky blue. Far from the flurry of motion bubbles and the cacophony of sub-aqua conversation, the old bull relaxes his swimming muscles, allows the ocean to take over.

After a few hours of aimless drifting, the whale finds the energy to spy-hop and punches his mounded skull above the surface to survey his surroundings. Out in the air, it is cloudless and crisp. In the distance, the wobbly horizon is blotted by stationary trawlers. The shore seems suddenly larger than usual. The whale can see clearly beyond the rutted cliffs and freckled beaches to the fringe of hazy green where the fields begin. He is deceived by the brightness and the blue and forgets that dusk will soon stamp the seabed into shadows and scatter the blank sky with pin-prick stars and puddles of timid moonlight. The old bull sinks back beneath the surface, sashays softly with the tide.

"Be-up be-up be-up be-up be-up be-up be-up be-up be-up..."

There is a gull treading air, barking like a broken car alarm. It is thinking that it might rest its wings and bob for a while before returning to the shore.

The whale emerges and replies, "Pppppphhhhhhhhhhooooooo sssssssssshhhhhhhhh."

Above water, through his blowhole, while lunging or breaching, all the whale has ever been able to say is: "Phoosh." Back underwater, he sings loudly in the dialect of his pod.

"Uurrrrrrrrrrrrrrrrrrrrrrrrrrkkkkkkkkkkkkkkkkkkkkkk urrrrrrkkkkkk."

The sound is hollow, tragic, the echo of a clarinet with a broken reed in an empty concert hall. The whale tries something a little more cheerful.

"Eeeeeeeeeeeepppppppppppppppppppp oup oup oup oup oup oup."

But the bird cannot understand. It circles a while longer, changes its mind, and flies away.

"Oup?"

Two bottle-nosed dolphins hear the whale. They spin through the water, chattering, whistling and clicking in a frenzy of friendliness. The old bull is aggravated by their spectacle of shimmies and twirls and flips, their hyperactive chirpiness, their pesky compassion. But when the dolphins tire of his reticence and glide away, the whale is engulfed by loneliness. He swims clumsily after them in the direction of the rocks.

When the whale sees lobster pots, he knows that the seabed is closer than it rightly should be. A few sorry lobsters tickle the criss-crossed bars of their cages with frondy antennae. A diminished shoal of smelt scamper past the whale, keeping a careful distance, looking glum and chilled. A conger eel crouches inside a broken bucket, poised to ambush anything of lesser genus. As the old bull approaches the sea shore, ribbons of slithery kelp tangle about his dorsal fin. He feels lassoed, defeated. Eventually the tips of his sickle-shaped flippers scuff the sand and throw small clouds of grit and shattered shell into his weary eyes.

"Oup," says the whale, sadly.

It is almost dark by the time he washes up on the beach. He blinks curiously at the trail of high tide: the mess of rusted beer cartons, faded buoys, swollen driftwood, all those eroded treasures the sea steals and weathers before vomiting them back up over the shore. The rubbish is dappled with shards of coloured plastic and broken glass and perfectly pebble-shaped chunks of polystyrene which have been carved and sculpted by the sea. There is a crushed red sandal with the buckle missing. There is a toy tea-cup, its pattern blanched into ghostliness. There is even a sodden Christmas tree buckled on its branches, last year's tinsel replaced by tendrils of bobbled bladder-wrack. Everything looks quite pretty to the feeble, fumbled whale, and so he concentrates on this prettiness as his blubber grows too tight and too warm, as the waves pull back and hiss away without him.

After five days, the beached whale explodes. The sound rips through the clear noon, the most extraordinary sound in all the world. The gulls rise up in fright. They drift cautiously on their outstretched wings. They yelp and bawl back down at the strangeness of the natural world.

Karma

Ursula co-ordinated the Senior Citizens' Parish Socials, and so the first thing that sprang to her mind in Doctor Brennan's clinic was what all the old biddies would say after she had called their bingo numbers, poured their tea and drifted out of their earshot to plate up custard creams, to butter fruit scones. She organised the whole thing – booking the community hall, recruiting the helpers, collecting all the nosey old ladies together. Once a week, every week, she fake smiled and fake laughed and cheerfully encouraged their reckless gossip-mongering. *If ever there has been a case of bad karma coming back to bite you*, Ursula thought, *this is it*.

But she immediately felt guilty for fretting about herself and her spotless reputation. While she was certainly set to suffer collateral flak, it was Vanessa who was taking the direct strike. Ursula stared at her youngest daughter where she lay on the examination table with her knees spread and her second chin slouching back into her flushed cheeks. Vanessa sucked and gulped and flapped like a salmon netted from the crest of a wave, floundering on the wooden deck, struggling for air.

"Oh Vanny."

Sniff sniff sniff blow gulp gulp blow.

"How can you not have known?"

Now that Vanessa was horizontal and exposed, it seemed as plain as day. The great rosy knoll of her stomach was taut and streaked. It stood in rigid contrast to the quivering handles that cascaded about it. Ursula coped with her daughter's joblessness, her fatness, her promiscuity. Yet she felt personally wounded by the tremendous stupidity that had carried Vanessa through almost seven months of pregnancy without even realising that a gestating human life was responsible for her suspicious indigestion and steadily expanding waistline. It was Ursula who ultimately wondered about her puking in the morning, who registered alarm bells at the absence of soiled tampons in the bathroom pedal-bin. It was Ursula who purchased the kit from the chemists, who coerced Vanessa into peeing on the stick, who insisted upon driving her to the clinic appointment.

"Why don't you come in again to talk properly in a day or two, once you've had some time to get used to the news?" Doctor Brennan said, kindly.

"Oh shit," Vanessa said, suddenly, desperately. "Ohshitohshitohshit-ohshitohshitohshit."

Then she sobbed all the way home. And as soon as they were past the front door, she shuffled to her bedroom and turned the key in the lock. It was then that Ursula realised it was up to her to tell everybody the horrible news, despite her own sketchy understanding of the circumstances. She lowered herself to a kitchen chair and remembered that on top of this there was still the whole of ordinary life demanding to continue. There was still the broken fridge and the elderly mother-in-law, the empty lunchboxes and the un-ironed washing, the gunky fish tank and the new kitten that sat in its litter tray scrabbling about amongst the silica pebbles, mewing helplessly.

By Saturday night, the tumult had hushed enough for Vanessa to escape from her bedroom. She stood on platform heels in the beer garden of Kavanagh's, propping up a picnic-bench with a pint of Bulmers in her left hand and a Marlboro in her right. Vanessa was not stupid so much as she was persuasive. She had worked hard to convince herself that the accidental foetus was not so, and now she was furious that biology had betrayed her; that in a matter of weeks her noncompliant body would spasm and churn and force her to push push push some unwanted new existence into the world. The view from the beer garden stretched beyond the soothing glow of the thatched pub to the gloomy fields for as far as Vanessa could see, and she knew that she was staring straight down the tunnel of her dismal destiny.

The morning the baby was born, Ursula could not find the kitten. She bundled Vanessa into the back seat in a duvet, her pyjama bottoms soaked in amniotic fluid and her hair all fluffed and mashed by sleep. When Ursula started the engine, she heard the whisper of a yowl and when she popped the hood, there it was. Half the flesh of its stomach had been torn away by the fan belt, the skin of its tail peeled back like a banana, but its eyes still looked up at her, its lungs still cried out.

"What is it, Mum?" Vanessa asked.

"Nothing to worry about," Ursula replied.

And then, halfway to the hospital Vanessa said, "Mum?"

"Yes, Vanny?"

"I'm sorry."

It was a Monday, and Ursula left the wounded kitten in a bloody heap on the lawn, and the baby was not fair of face like the nursery rhyme promised. Its head was eerily small, and its top lip shrank away to a gaping hollow in its palate, and its stunted little brain made it glassy-eyed and placid. But its heart pounded stubbornly, and it whimpered in tune with the hum of its breathing apparatus, and it stared up through the glass roof of its incubator, determined to survive and ruin all their lives.

Darren David Koolman

Solifuge

For an average of five hours per day –
And that is roughly one fifth of my life –
I will thrive in an unlit sanctuary.

For an average of five hours per day,
My aphelion will be under the clay –
There, by my own resplendence, I'll survive –

For an average of five hours per day –
And that is roughly one fifth of my life.

Amaranth

*The Blessing of him that was ready to perish came upon me;
and I caused the widow's heart to sing for joy.*

                                        The Book of Job

Remember when he conjured you a rose,
And haled your drooping cheek to amaranth?
I felt the frisson in your relic hand –
The glinting tears he kissed as he proposed.

Now, you parch your eyes in the charnel house,
Affecting marble in a sackcloth tent:
A desert weeps since you will not lament;
A simoom squalls unslaked by stolen drouths.

Why drown your husband daily in the sand?
Why wimple grief in a marmoreal frown?
Time does not reckon *love* its carrion –
What beaks the flesh will leave a flower to stand!

Your love decays when flesh to flesh it cleaves,
So pour your eyes upon these withered leaves.

On Reading a Biography of Shakespeare

...All is yellow to the jaundiced eye.
                                    Pope

Schools of dumb presagers are gathered in seas
To structure a temple on water.

In a rag-and-bone box he lies
Mute.

Death's outlet song
Unsung.

Imagine

A love's might body him forth
As springing sinews interweave.

Skin and hair enfolding bone –
Curtains raised and burning globes.

The black ink of many friars
Banish shadows bleached by time.

The cordate peal of celestial fires
Resounding Mercy, Pity, Love.

Then through the cloud of a shattered casket
From the stygian void
He flounces

To stride the earth with naked feet
And shake a masquerading quill.

The rest is noise

Of thrashing waves and leaden clouds
And black swan jeremiads.

Of aimless barks on jaundiced seas
Canting for elusive peers

Rain

Iridescent creeds
Unseam in the dismantling
Of a raining sun

That blinks on the verge
A searing eye as garnets
Curl the niggard sky.

Consider the earth.

Being nourished by heaven's dust

She horripilates
A hummock of skulls

As the foot of Antaeus
Impresses
A sole

Mirabile Dictu

My toe percusses the escritoire,
While the ratamacue of my pen
Disperses the silence of a thoughtless
Brain – but then, a versicoloured friend
Comes tumbling in, unsteady on a
Wavering wind, and settles on the pen.

Welcoming the distraction,
I globe her in my hands –
An uninspired epigone.
The usual obeisance.

Not tickling my palms to fan my thoughts,
She flaps insouciantly – while I furrow
Grand things to write on ephemerality,
And death and time – and other themes already
Wrought in a billion other minds.

Argument Against Thesauruses

Seeming alike –
Together thrown –
The seeds of philology
Are sown –

Harmless drudges
Furrowed ruts –
But coffles of poets harvest
The fruits –

Helots lost in
A wilderness –
They rifle Pluto's garden
For a verse –

Reaping for leaves
Of bay and thyme –
To defalcate their coinage
In a Rime –

"…he made the stars also."

Evening and morning.

A glooming dawn.

The stars are drowning still.

I have learned not to blench at shadows.

I have learned how to be a shadow.

Though aspiring fingers occlude the stars.

How many more tomorrows?

The God of Boethius skips to the last page.

A coruscating hand

Anna Smith

Choose Your Own
Adventure

You are Melanie Bouchard, 26. You work in the admin department at the BC Provincial Government, and live in Metchosin, BC, a rural suburb of Victoria whose name in Coast Salish means "stinking fish." You're single. Your last vacation was five years ago, at the end of your undergrad, to Crete – there, you drank ouzo, lay in the sun, danced, bungee-jumped, slept with an unsatisfying Greek man and contracted gonorrhoea. You came home three days early.

The year is 2009, the season, summer. Pittsburgh just won the Stanley Cup and all anyone can talk about is the kid from Cole Harbour, Sidney Crosby, number 87. The next Wayne Gretzky, everyone's saying. The last Wayne Gretzky, pointy-headed Wayne-o himself, is on TV hawking drill bits and golf shirts. The thermometer hasn't dropped below thirty-five in a week. You don't have air-conditioning.

You are at work.

The adventure begins – turn to page one to start!

You sit in an office cubicle on the third floor. You file. You shred. Your feet have swollen in the heat so that your shoes feel much too tight but you are in the final stretch of the day, the last half-hour before you can go home and watch *Project Runway* in peace. The sun streams in through the window across the corridor. Your co-worker, Mandy, is talking about her boyfriend. Again.

"He says he's working late," she says, "but last night he didn't get home until three and he didn't pick up when I called. Do you think he's cheating?"

Yes, you think. "No," you say. "No, Brad would never do that."

"Even if I called his office phone and he says he was working so hard he didn't even hear it?"

"So he didn't hear it," you say.

Mandy is silent for a moment. You file. You shred. "He seemed so angry too, when I asked."

You swallow some instinct which makes you want to say what you know you shouldn't, and wonder what it is about lying that makes it seem like it is good, and what it is about women that makes them seem like they should lie. You settle for a thing that is not true but that may not be wholly false. "Brad loves you," you say. "What you do with that is up to you."

Mandy brightens. "Last winter he was acting all serious and secretive too, Melanie, like you would not believe and I was so, so sad that he didn't want to be with me any more and then one day he came home with tickets to Jamaica and he said that that was why he was acting so strange, was that he didn't want to ruin the surprise."

It's 4:57. You file. You shred. "That's fantastic," you say. You say: "Wow."

"He's the sweetest," Mandy says. She turns off her monitor and uses her reflection in the black screen to touch up her lipstick. "Thanks, Mel."

"No problem," you say, and you wonder what the problem is with you, that now suddenly you want to correct her, to tell her how sweet Brad probably isn't and that he's cheating, maybe, though you have no proof and you've only met Brad once, at a company picnic, and when you saw him you thought: This is it? And then felt so badly for thinking it that you flirted with him all day and Mandy wouldn't talk to you for a week. "Any time," you say. It's 5:01. You turn off your computer. You hobble to the car.

Driving, barefoot, with your stockings balled in a corner on the back seat and your hateful shoes under the passenger seat, you see the turnoff for the ferries. California, you think, suddenly. It's no Jamaica and there will be no Brad but who needs Brad – instead there will be beaches full of college boys with sand in their hair. There will be flip-flops. There will be tans and long nights and your hands will lose the dry roughness they get from touching all this useless paper. You haven't looked at a document you filed or shredded since 2006, 2007 maybe. You don't need to look at these. There is money in your bank account.

If you drive to California, turn to page four
If you go to Costco and buy a frozen pizza, turn to page eight

You put the pizza in the oven and pour a glass of orange juice. You think for a second about adding a shot of vodka and the thought scares you a little even though you don't do it. You live alone.

While the pizza heats you turn on your computer, though you're sick to death of staring at screens, and open an Internet window. You have all the Victoria job boards' quirkiest job types bookmarked. The volunteer fire department is recruiting: men and women with a high level of fitness required immediately, first aid and CPR mandatory. Will train.

The heat wave isn't stopping and half the province is dead wood anyway with the pine beetle infestation, all so much tinder. The fires two years ago burned within a block of the Kelowna strip malls, a city the size of your own and not much drier. You look out the window at the lawn, crisped brown and dry as corn husks. This is Metchosin, land of hobby farms and hippies and wood. If the forest went up they would all be evacuated, and overworked firefighters would do "everything they could." This is a town of whitewash and sagging eaves troughs. This is not Victoria. This is not Kelowna, even.

You remember when you were seven and living out east, and a tornado passed within a kilometre of your house. Your mother woke you all up, your brothers and sister and you, and took you down to the basement with blankets and flashlights and boxes of cookies even though it was later than you had ever been awake. Outside you could hear the big tree scraping against the car port and rain lashing down like it had been thrown, and all the windows in the house were bowing and rattling against the wind. When she went to wake your father, he only grunted and rolled over and said, "Is the tornado in the house?" Of course not, she said, and you could hear her all the way from the basement, though it was years before she told you what he'd said to put that note into her voice. "Wake me up when it's in the house," he said, and she left him to it and came downstairs and told you to stop eating cookies and go to sleep already; it was late and we might all be on the street tomorrow.

The next day though you weren't all on the street, you were pointing your house out on the news, excited, when they showed the path the tornado had taken, and your mother was shaking, and outside the street was filled with clean-up crews. They were fast-moving, efficient, like the teamwork teams on *Reading Rainbow*, and they had a camaraderie that you recognised even then, a sense of being in this together, of helping others and being helpful and being strong. Half of BC is a tinderbox and there aren't enough firefighters to go around and people's homes and basements and fathers are at risk, you think. You do have CPR.

IF YOU APPLY TO BECOME A VOLUNTEER FIREFIGHTER, TURN TO PAGE SEVENTEEN

IF YOU PUT ON 'PROJECT RUNWAY,' TURN TO PAGE FORTY-ONE

The oven has made the heat in the house almost unbearable. You open all the windows and your blouse, and lie under the coffee table eating pizza and wishing it was popsicles. The new *Project Runway* doesn't start for an hour but you have last week's still saved on your TiVo and you watch it again because it's hot outside. You think about that old Joni Mitchell song about the hissing of summer lawns and the squinting sun. You could die here tomorrow and nobody would find you for a week.

The phone rings. It's Ellie, your sister. She's in Chicago on business and her husband Alex is at home. He can't get the house alarm to turn off or the air-conditioning to turn on. It's killing him, she says.

"I thought men were supposed to be good at that kind of shit," you say.

"Have you met Alex?" she says.

IF YOU GO HELP ALEX, TURN TO PAGE FORTY-FIVE

IF YOU LIE UNDER THE COFFEE TABLE WAITING TO DIE, TURN TO PAGE THIRTY-TWO

You have never been to Ellie's house before when Ellie wasn't in it, never even to return a roasting pan or to drop in for coffee. You wonder if Alex has ever opened the door to you, though when you think it, it seems ridiculous and you guess he must have some time.

He opens the door today and you hear the alarm right away, the kind of shrill noise that eats into your skull. Alex comes out onto the porch and closes the door after him and the noise goes down a little, but only a little.

"Isn't the whole point of those things that when they go off the cops come?" you ask.

"The company called," Alex says, and he rubs the back of his neck with one hand. He is wearing sweat pants that bag around his knees and a T-shirt with a cartoon of a bobble-headed Sidney Crosby facing off against a square-jawed Alexei Ovetchkin, Lord Stanley's glistening trophy in the background. The caption underneath reads, "TWO GIRLS – ONE CUP." "I could answer all their questions so they said to just turn it off. They said did I want them to send a guy but I said no." He grins guiltily. "Guess I should've said yes, eh." He coughs into his chest and rubs his head again. There are sweat stains under his armpits that reach halfway to his waist. "They said I just had to punch in the code."

You roll your eyes. "Show me where," you say.

Alex shrugs. You find it. The code is his birthday.

While you're at it, you find the air-conditioning for him too, and set it to cold cold cold cold cold, even though you know that's wasteful. You go around the house and close all the windows with him and he follows you into his and Ellie's bedroom, which up 'til right now you've only ever thought of as Ellie's bedroom, and your breath catches in your chest a little.

"Do you have to go soon?" he says, and you think he sounds a little mournful.

"Yeah," you say. The bed is made but lumpy, like all the feathers in the duvet are down at one end. Alex is standing between you and the air vent and he smells musky. "Yeah," you say, "I should go."

But you have nowhere to go. To the mall, if it's open. To a bar.

IF YOU GO TO THE BAR, TURN TO PAGE EIGHTY-NINE

IF YOU STAY WITH ALEX, TURN TO PAGE SEVENTY-TWO

You order a drink and sit. This is not the same as vodka in your orange juice, you think – this is constructively putting yourself out there, looking around, plenty of fish in the sea. You have gone to bars before with girl-friends, looking to get picked up, but you never meet anyone that way – you look too unapproachable, too complete. You wonder if like this you look too vulnerable. You wonder if you're sending the right signals. You try to think of yourself as the kind of tough woman who can shoot a gun and drinks alone in bars because she likes to.

The night goes on and, though there are men in the bar, all in white button-up shirts or T's the colour of the California sea, their eyes flick to you and then away. Dating is a sophisticated game of wink murder, you think.

There is a man at the bar – a boy, almost. He can't be more than twenty-two. Yet when you were in Greece, the man that you went home with was the same age you are now and you were no older than this guy anyway, all sand-coloured hair and the sleeves of his T-shirt tight around his arms. He looks your way and his eyes don't flick onwards. You are seized with the desire to wink.

IF YOU HAVE A DRINK SENT ALONG TO HIM, A MARTINI MAYBE, LIKE THE KIND OF TOUGH AMERICAN BROAD WHO CAN SHOOT A GUN AND DRINKS ALONE BECAUSE SHE LIKES TO, TURN TO PAGE ONE HUNDRED AND ONE

IF YOU TALK TO THE BOY, TURN TO PAGE NINETY-SEVEN

You bring your drink with you, and wonder if you should have one for him too but he's already holding a sleeve of some light-coloured beer that's full almost to the top. He glances over as you approach, smiles warmly but looks away again. You smile back but already he's gone.

"How much does a polar bear weigh," you say.

He turns back and looks at you but he doesn't turn fast and there's a look on his face, the kind of slight smile people give you when you speak a language that they don't. There is music in the bar. You wonder if he heard you. "Excuse me?" he says.

"Do you know what time it is?" you ask.

He smiles again, shrugs and gets out his phone. "It's ten thirty," he says. He goes to put his phone away.

"Want to put my number in there while you've got that out?" you say. You blurt.

He angles his body away from yours. "I think you might be a little drunk," he says.

"I am," you say. "I'm little and I'm drunk. Only a little drunk though. Only not enough drunk."

You swill back what's left of your cocktail and put the glass down too hard on the bar. You order another and go back to your table and wink over your shoulder while you're leaving, though the boy is looking another way and all the muscles of your face feel tight. You drink the new cocktail too fast, even though you don't really want it, you just want to get out of the bar. There is only one decent bar in Metchosin, out by the Motel 8 and not far from the highway, and now you've ruined it for yourself because you think you can feel everyone's eyes on you, even though you've never met them and anyway, they aren't looking.

The last time you were this drunk was at Ellie's wedding, because Ellie is two and a half years younger than you and Alex high-fived his best man when he signed the register and Ellie wanted to high-five you as the maid of honour too and you let your fingers brush her palm because she was your sister, but that's all. Alex played duffers hockey, had played for years as a junior and played well, had met Sidney Crosby and said he was a dickhead. Alex still had pecs. At the reception the best man had told a story about the time Ellie had driven into town to change the spark plugs in Alex's truck, and he'd known that it was love. You told the story about the first time you met Alex, and halfway through you wondered if you were giving things away that you shouldn't. You think about calling him. You decide you won't call him. You decide that that would be crazy, and bitchy, and that you love your sister and that the sea is full of fish.

IF YOU CALL ALEX, TURN TO PAGE ONE HUNDRED TEN

"Are you still up?" you say. "There's no air-conditioning at my place. There's no way I'm getting to sleep there tonight."

"I'm up," he says, and he sounds a little cautious.

You scratch the steering wheel with your index finger. You shouldn't drive, you know it, but all the cops will be at the beaches on a night like this and good luck getting a taxi. "Can I come?" you say.

You hear Alex on the other end of the phone breathing a little too loud. "Sure," he says. "You can come sleep in the spare room."

You won't sleep in the spare room. You know it. When you get to the door, Alex has changed into a white T-shirt that stretches around his biceps and jeans that sit just so on his hips. He is sweating, although the house is cold. There are goosebumps on his arms. "Hey," he says.

"Hey," you say. You walk in past him and into the kitchen. You find yourself walking from the hips the way you did in junior high when you wanted to look sophisticated, or in college when you wanted to look drunk. He follows you in and opens the fridge.

"You want something?" he says, like a man who doesn't know how a thing like this might start.

"Whiskey," you say. He closes the fridge. There is whiskey in the cupboard over the oven.

"There's no ice," he says.

"Straight is fine," you say. He pours.

He brings you the drink and stands a little bit too close to you. You can see the pulsing of the vein in his neck and the pucker in his T-shirt where his nipples might be. You shift your weight a half-inch closer. He touches your arm, and then moves away.

"How's work?" he asks.

He sits in a straight-backed chair with his whiskey on his thigh and fidgets with the sleeve of his T-shirt. Every part of him is straight, stiff. His feet even are lined up exactly with the chair legs, strangely vulnerable in just white cotton socks. You take off your shoes.

"It's work," you say. Your heart is beating fast. You remember the first time you met Alex, how he was still playing a little, even though even he knew by then that he was on his way down. You were at a concert with Ellie and he came to stand behind you both, between you. He was wearing a white shirt and blue jeans and had the longest eyelashes you had ever seen in your whole life. You had just graduated, just broken up with your college boyfriend, just booked an impulsive ticket to Athens, leaving in a week. This is it, you'd thought. This is the one. "Is this spot taken?" he had asked, though it wasn't a spot. "Sure," you had said. "Come anytime."

"When will Ellie be back," you say.

"Tuesday," Alex says. He throws back his whiskey in one gulp and looks at you, right at you.

"I'll turn the air-conditioning down," you say. "You must be freezing." You reach out, awkward, and put the back of your hand against the back of his neck as though you were checking, although why would you check? He doesn't move away, though there is something in his face that you can't define. You are very drunk. You tuck your fingers into the back of his shirt collar. "Unless you like it cold," you say. You touch the coarse hairs at the back of his neck and he sags a little, and stands up, close.

IF YOU SLEEP WITH YOUR SISTER'S HUSBAND, TURN TO PAGE ONE HUNDRED TWENTY-ONE

Eddie Naessens

Somebody's Boy

I'm driving the scenic route home from Dublin to Kilkenny. The sky is petrol blue and the evening sun lights up patches of high cloud, casting orangey and lilac hues over the gorse and heather around the Sugar Loaf Mountain. I check the fuel gauge and relax when I see there's enough to get me home.

I spent the afternoon helping my eldest son move into his flat; he starts college tomorrow. For months I've been telling his mother not to worry and promised not to give him advice, but she's smart enough to know it's myself I'm trying to convince, and that my promise not to give advice is as broken as the ones I made to get fit, tidy the garage, and learn Spanish.

My own father's words come back to gently mock me. He was right. I didn't notice time fly – and now I'm the old geezer in the Wicklow hills at sunset talking to himself in a car that needs a service, on a road that needs more cat's eyes, remembering squalid and happy days when I thought of a future where I would not become my father. I'm in that future now, looking through the rear-view mirror, reflecting – on my years in flatland, and the story I cannot tell my son.

In summer 1988, Dublin was a thousand years old and I was on the lookout for a new place to live. After three desperate weeks of viewing grubby firetraps, I got word of a place that sounded liveable so I went to see it, half in hope and half-prepared for yet more disappointment. The street was lined with trees and in the evening light looked almost Parisian; a perfect contrast to the landlady, Mrs. Mooney. The flat itself was the top floor of a Georgian house between the canal and St. Stephen's Green – getting up to it was a workout in itself. As I caught my breath, I began to notice the little things that could make the place home. The hallway had a skylight, and the kitchen – though it was a medley of Formica, jaded lino, and flimsy furniture – had views of the Grand Canal, church spires, and the Dublin Mountains. There was also a bathroom, and three bedrooms of varying sizes. I picked the low-ceilinged bedroom next to the kitchen, which had wooden slats along the dividing wall, a bed, a school desk, a set of drawers, and a threadbare carpet tacked over loose floorboards. When it was windy outside, that room creaked like an old timber frigate.

I moved in before the August bank holiday and for a few weeks, the other two bedrooms remained empty. However, a returning tide of flat-hunting students soon traipsed through the place guided by the shrill-voiced Mrs. Mooney. It seemed as if she was waiting for the moment when I took the first forkful of my dinner before she brought these glum strangers to the kitchen. "And this is the kitchen-cum-living-room in here, there's the sink, the fridge, and Conor – he's living here. And over here is the oven and grill."

One evening she called up the stairs. "Conor, are you home?" Whether I was or not, she was coming in.

"Sorry to disturb you," she said, stepping into the kitchen. "Conor, this is Derek Bunyan."

Was this one of my new flatmates? Would I have to share a kitchen, a hallway, and a bathroom with this stocky stranger? He was wearing a striped shirt and floral tie, a V-necked sweater with a diamond pattern, and a beige Crombie coat. The shirt collar was too small for him. His brown hair was neatly parted and he had a small, hairy mole in front of his right ear.

Mrs. Mooney then introduced me, "Conor is an actor."

"Oh really?" said Derek, with a polite smile.

"Do you ever watch *Crime Catchers*, Derek?" she asked him.

"No, not really," he replied.

"But you know the programme I'm talking about – it does all that stuff about crime?"

"Yeah, I know it, I just don't watch it."

"Well, Conor was on it last year, isn't that right, Conor?"

"Ah... yeah," I said.

"You don't mind me telling Derek that you're famous?"

"No, you're fine," I lied.

"He was a robber jumping over a counter... did you see it?"

"I might have," said Derek, faking a vague memory, "but I don't really watch that programme, Mrs. Mooney. To be honest, I'm usually too busy."

She turned to me, and in a hushed tone she said, "Derek is going into second-year Business Studies in... was it Trinity or UCD you said you were?"

"UCD," he said.

"UCD, that's it," she said. "I knew it was either one or the other."

Derek moved in that weekend, and on Sunday he asked to borrow milk until he got to the supermarket on Monday.

"It's just," he said, "that shop at the junction's a fierce rip-off."

"Take whatever you like," I said.

He didn't return the milk on Monday. Instead, he marked the milk he had bought with a yellow Post-It label and took over the lower shelf in the cupboard for his own food and moved mine to the shelf above.

Later that week, Lizzy and Rachel moved into the larger, remaining room. Lizzy, from Sligo, was studying Sociology and Art History. She had fair skin, rosy cheeks, green eyes, and wore a tie-dyed bandana and a nose stud that glinted whenever she moved her head.

Rachel, an exchange student from New York, was pint-sized and gregarious. She revelled in telling stories of her everyday experiences in

Dublin, and took to making the flat more homely. As the days shortened, she did battle with the grot. Flowers and plants appeared. She replaced the cruddy kitchen bin with a shiny flip-top one, covered the shabby furnishings with tasteful fabrics, dumped the slimy-grey shower curtain and hung an expensive coloured one with an image by Mondrian in its place. By Halloween the flat was almost chic.

While Lizzy and I were happy to help out, Derek only sneered at each improvement. "Flowers! Christ! Makes the place look like a feckin' funeral home. Good luck with trying to get your deposit back. I'm not sure Mrs. Mooney will be too happy with you throwing out her bin. I can't believe anyone would pay that much for a shower curtain – what was wrong with the one we had?"

The girls were easy to get along with. We had dinner together about twice a week. As we prepared dinner one evening in November, we discussed the Derek problem. Perhaps his sarcasm was an attempt at humour or perhaps he was just awkward; he didn't have a lot to say for himself except when he wanted to "borrow" never-to-be-returned food. But whatever the reasons, we decided to ask him to chip in and make an effort. It was hard to know where to start. The electric bill seemed like a neutral starting point. But there were less pleasant things too. He rarely washed anything, left bowls of sticky muesli and pots with dried-in food piled in the sink, and kept almost-empty cups of coffee in his room long enough for mould spores to bloom, at which point he'd leave them on the kitchen table. He licked spoons before dipping them back into someone else's jam, never replaced what he took, and avoided any discussion of paying for general household things.

As we started dinner, he arrived.

"Christ, what a day!" he said, crossing over to the fridge. "Jesus, what the hell are you eating?"

"It's Mexican," said Lizzy, pulling an extra chair to the table. "Like to try some?"

"Nah!" he said, scrunching his face in disgust.

"What, you don't like Mexican?" Rachel said.

"Nah, it's feckin' peasant food – fullov chilli and shit?" He put back on his jacket and left, returning twenty minutes later with a steak and kidney pie. He ate at the table while we had dessert. He left the brown paper bag and the foil tray on the table. As he got up to leave, I called him back. "Derek," I said, "can you hang on for a sec, we need to sort out some stuff."

At first he agreed to pay for his quarter of the electricity but became defensive when Lizzy pointed out the mess he had left on the table.

"It's only a bag and some tinfoil," he said. "Sure, what else would you women be doing?"

"Sorry, Derek, is that your idea of humour?" asked Rachel.

Then he gave me a sly wink, "Christ, this is the problem with Arts students, eh Conor?"

"Come off it, Derek," I said. "You haven't done a tap since you got here."

"What do you mean like?"

"You haven't done anything since you moved in here."

"I'm busy!"

"We're all busy, Derek," said Lizzy.

"Oh, come on, don't give me that," Derek said, leaning back and folding his arms, "You're farting around college, shopping, and in pubs."

Rachel jumped in: "Guys, cool it. This is going nowhere. Derek, we're talking about everyone paying their share and keeping our home –"

"This isn't my home," he said.

"What's that supposed to mean?" Rachel asked.

"Well, I'm hardly ever here."

"That's bullshit, Derek," said Rachel.

He trotted out reasons why he should not have to share the bills equally. On paying for loo roll, he insisted, "I get all the loo roll I need at college," and argued that because he went home at weekends and spent most of his time out of the flat he should not have to pay so much for electricity. On the matter of cleaning dishes, he argued that it was wasteful to wash single cups and plates, and added, "I'm studying

Business Management. I know a lot more about these things. Doing dishes is good practice for actors and Arts students, I'm really preparing you for what you'll be doing when you're fully qualified!"

Being Irish, Lizzy and me thought Derek was simply "an ignorant, tight-arsed, eejit." Rachel, however, had a more explanatory view. She concluded that Derek's behaviour showed all the signs of mild social anxiety coupled with compensating passive aggression and mild contempt. She suggested that since we had to put up with him, we should "contain our frustrations and try, somehow, to include him." She had done therapy and she spoke about the things the Irish generally drown in drink. She talked such a good game that Lizzy agreed with her analysis but disagreed on how to deal with the problem as framed. Yet, for all their ideas on psychosocial dynamics and problem-solving methodology, they expected me to sort out the problems with both Derek and the flat.

When we came back after the Christmas break, Mrs. Mooney's husband, Terrence, began sub-dividing some larger flats into smaller units. For three noisy and dusty weeks in January, he vandalised four new bedsits into the building. The consequences of these alterations became apparent when the new tenants moved in. Our water pressure dropped, the electric shower burned out, and the electrics failed. On the plus side, it defrosted our fridge, returning a long-lost bag of oven chips.

A week later, we became aware of a more serious problem. It started with tiny noises in the walls, little gallops, and fitful scratching. It brought us all closer, and even Derek came to discuss the problem with us; it seemed, for a time, we were united against a common enemy.

I got back from rehearsals one afternoon to find the girls in the kitchen looking through the rental section of the evening paper. They were moving out and asked if I would join them. I had part-time work as a hospital orderly that just about paid me enough to allow me do some acting work. So, I knew the flat was the best I could afford. I'd been in Dublin long enough to have seen the horrors behind the small ads: damp basements with bars on the windows, that reeking stench of must, electricity meters that charged triple the price, and the grim queuing in the rain for the chance to live in some cute hoor's cash cow.

We made tea but had run out of biscuits. Rachel went to the cupboard and took out an unopened packet of chocolate digestives belonging to Derek.

"Hey, Lizzy," she said, dangling the packet, "care for one of Derek's cookies?"

Lizzy shook her head. "Better not."

"Oh, come on," said Rachel. "Don't be so frickin' ethical."

"It's nothing to do with ethics, I just don't want..."

"What! Stop the press!" Rachel teased, "'Lizzy Keegan Refuses Cookie!'"

"Put them back," said Lizzy, "I'm sick of having arguments with that arsehole."

"You're moving out – what difference does it make?"

"It makes a difference to me; I don't want to stoop to his level. That's all."

"Oh, come on, Lizzy!" said Rachel. "Can you believe this girl?" she asked me, and placed the packet in front of Lizzy.

Lizzy picked up the packet and put it back in the cupboard. I took it out again, nibbled at the base of the packet, before placing it back on the shelf.

"You evil bastard," Rachel said, "I can't believe you've just done that. Well done!"

When Derek came in, he switched on the kettle, checked the fridge for milk, knowing he had left none there that morning, and finally, went to the cupboard.

"Whoa!" he yelped. "Feckin' mice!" He fired the packet into the bin. From the stairs he shouted back out, "Can someone switch off that kettle!" Lizzy switched off the kettle, and when the front door closed, I reached into the bin and retrieved the biscuits.

The motorbike courier must have been looking to his right, down the junction into Earlsfort Terrace where the traffic comes from town. That is how I've pictured it. He sped into the bus lane, didn't see Derek. Derek certainly didn't see him. He was probably rooting in his pockets for change, or figuring out how a mouse had climbed up to his biscuits.

I've been thinking about it a long time. I see him spinning through the air, his skull smacking onto the road and his forehead cracking off the footpath. His face had to be reconstructed; the mortician did a good job.

One of my workmates from the hospital drove us down to the removal. We walked in the cortège, shook hands with his family in the church, and listened to the priest talk about the contingency of life, the twists of fate, and the importance of faith.

At their house, Derek's parents went out of their way to make sure we were looked after for food and drink. Their drink seemed to have no effect on me. I smoked what cigarettes I had and got a few more from Derek's sister. His parents kept thanking us for being so kind to Derek; he had spoken very highly of us to them. They told us we were much nicer than the people he lived with in first year. His mother spoke serenely.

"It's just awful what young people have to go through," she said. She kept telling us about Derek being a home bird. She was desperate to tell us about him, she struggled for words, and at one point, apologised for speaking about him in the present tense. Then she cried. His father, a big soft-faced man, brought us into the kitchen.

"Make sure and eat whatever you do," he said, "there's plenty in it."

Eleanor Hooker

Three Things

Three things I keep secure: my life, my truth, my boys.
As I contemplate the surface of the lake,
Three things I long to lose: my doubts, my fears, their lies.

And so I dive. Through underwater gloom, pike eyes
Find me, their torn mouths lipstick-stained. Make no mistake,
Three things I keep secure: my life, my truth, my boys.

Four times, four times ago, pike bit through my cries, dyed
My heart ink black, hands fish-scaled, tattooed 'til I ached
To lose three things at last: my doubts, my fears, their lies.

I cannot keep or lose it all, nor mollify
The pike, whose teeth grow from clenched fists. For their sake,
These things I've kept secure: my life, my truth, my boys,

For even when they're dead, razor-toothed pike will try
To swallow whole, attempt to gut their prey, to rake
Through things I long to lose: my doubts, my fears, their lies.

Lock it down inside ink stains, sketch it inside joy,
So when the pike swims close, he'll never ever take
Three things I've kept secure: my life, my truth, my boys,
Just things I long to lose: my doubts, my fears, their lies.

Glow Stone

Hurtling past moon day's unmade fields, past all
Those wasted hours farther back the same train.
Getting up to find you, a stricken trawl
Through storybook days, damped with fretful rain.
The same train, but your car grappled back to
Yesterday. I managed just to ravel
Time as it spliced my need to nurture you.
How could I let this happen, to travel
Down the same lines as my parents?
Listen to me child, this is not the worst,
Please allow a moment for atonement,
We'll snatch a piece of nevermore, but first,
Entrust me with that glow stone love, to creel
For night the light of day, a moon day's steal.

Granddad

for Dad

And especially when red angels lit
From his pipe and set his chest aglow
With rubies, did I love my Granddad,
In the holiest clothes in all the land.

When Hamlet's spectre flickered
At the edges, and bleak school rain
Thrashed our house, and Granddad
Spelled "*sure*" when asked for "*shur*"

And I didn't correct for the love of him.
When Mother and sister breathed
"*Nell! he's gone*" and Granddad still –
Beside me, and brother sketched

Him on old brown paper, 'til Granddad
Lunged a green-filled cough at those
Who thought he'd gone and almost
Measured. When stories of Kerry

And the Hunger and the Troubles
Made of him a giant, *illness* shrank
Him back. And when at last he left
His tales behind, he was the first dead

I'd ever seen. I longed to lift
That yellow sunken, unsmiling face
To find the man who whispered
"*faith faith*", when red angels set
His chest aglow with rubies.

Nailed Down

That sacred space between words is commensurate
with loss. It's true. Nailed down it pegs
love, hate too for that matter.
Why, look at the space
between
you
and
and
and
and
and
m
e.

Shadows

In a city crowd, darkened by shadows, ragged and broken,
Nothing stirred that did not reveal itself, and all the while
Voices mumbling in my head were whispered words unspoken.

The footless man in clown's shoes lay Dublin'd down and stricken
In the ditches of his mind, his fading star too febrile
For a city crowd, darkened by shadows, ragged and broken.

Hear the deaf girl signing to her herself, her hands true tokens
Of the words her moving lips could never say, eyes that smile
At voices mumbling in her head, at whispered words unspoken.

Metal tears leak from the ears of suited men, heartbroken
By the cold exchange of talk to spectral beings, more exiles
In a city crowd, darkened by shadows, ragged and broken.

Such scenes play out the strained chords of life. When I am woken
From these inky dreams of writing down our lives, will I rile
The voices in my head, the whispered words unspoken,

Or can I weave the stuff of "heavens' treasured cloths", ridden
With the threads of "light and half-light", misshaped and styled
By a city crowd, darkened by shadows, ragged and broken,
By voices mumbling in my head, by whispered words unspoken?

Afternoon Tea

Afternoon tea, four p.m. in her lair. Polish, gilt, flair, all illusion. Decay reeking
on her breath, the air besmirched by her rot. Inclined to better view her
clawed feet, she strains the tea through your deaf ear. A drip-drop
drip-drop drumming through your skull. You look away but
catch her eye double-blinking in your hand. Roll it to
and fro. Used pike teeth form her iris, her
reflections sneer and mock you. Wrung
out, she mops a spill with your freshly
laundered beating heart. Her brew is
full of lies, made yours now too,
it was sifted through your life
remember? Time to go.
"A photograph before you leave, my dear."
Your soul snapped... and framed... and hung.

Breathing Lessons

Can you breathe better now?

...as she sucks all the air from your lungs
and binds you in her purple vice of demands.

Hold still, let me drive this rusty nail through
Your breast, scratch a hex on your heart.

Can you breathe better now?

You don't need this arm, it's greedy, selfish
Of you to want two. Let me twist it off.

Let me saw you in half; you were never
Whole anyway. See how I help you, doll?

Can you breathe better now?

Melting Lead

I've heard it all my life. Pull up
A chair inside yourself and listen.

A gland in your neck will make
Your eyes pulsate, bulge with malignant staring.

Pull up a chair inside yourself and listen. Listen
To a tale of lead hands melting.

A westerly with jagged teeth snaps a beech
In two. Lead hands melt inside its hollowed core.

A fallen tree sounds the air if ears will hear
Its cracking bones. Leaden hands will cannibalise

The bellied trunk for firewood. Pull up a chair
Inside yourself and listen as a fractured stump

Wounds the earth, and wounded earth sifts root
From shallow ground. A pyre ablaze will burn

For days, a spectral beacon at the water's edge. Lead hands
Melted down to liquid silver pouring into the world,

A blister at its centre, cave bled to its heart. Pull up
A chair inside yourself and listen as your hollowed core

Is filled with leaden hands, molten leaden hands
Filling the empty centre at your heart.

Pull up a chair inside yourself and listen.

Steven Louie

Gloves and Slippers

This is how I remember it happening before I started losing things – before I started leaving doors open and drying my eyes on the bed sheets and pillowcases, before I started forgetting people and words and how to put words to people. I asked Mr. Frink, who teaches Science, to help me understand. I asked him why parts of me were shutting down and going blank. I asked him why I forgot things. He explained electric circuits, how currents flow and how they become disconnected before they go dark.

It was the last time I would ever play stickball with my brother, Charlie. We played in the alley down beneath the gangway, next to the courtyard behind my family's three-storey brownstone on the North Side of Chicago. I was younger, so it was usually my brother's friends who came over, and I liked being allowed to hang with the older boys. It made me feel like less of an outsider. Charlie had a bent for rebellion. He always liked doing things our father wished us not to. He sometimes took Dad's baseball glove from the desk in the third-storey study, even though we weren't allowed to go there because that's where Dad did his work and played old records. Dad loved that glove. He used to oil it on the couch, watching *True Grit*, working the old, stiff leather, trying to rub youth back into it.

But Charlie didn't care about that, because he hadn't begun to lose things yet. We played in the alley for hours, with our own rules, and our own hands, and Dad's glove; the leather that my brother convinced me had come from humans, like the mummies we saw at the Museum of Natural History, dried skin pulled tight around the bends and curves of their bones. I thought about how many people had become baseball gloves, and what kind of glove I might become.

It rained hard that day, but we played anyway. The hard rain rattled off skylights in the den, and the unused flowerpots on the deck were pooled with rainwater. Charlie grabbed the glove from the study and headed for the door. I followed, racing as usual, Charlie in front and me behind. We ran out the back door, through the entryway, where Mom used to hang our coats and stack our shoes after we would leave them lying around on couches and on the backs of chairs. Charlie barged through the flimsy storm door and leapt onto the deck. I followed him through, before the door slammed shut, and halfway down the iron steps to the alley, I tried to pass him at the turn. I remember feeling oddly aware of myself, as if for the first time I would pass Charlie by, I would be best at something. But then my foot slipped on the slick metal landing. As I fell, I reached out for Charlie's arm to steady myself, but I grabbed hold of Dad's glove instead, and pulled it from Charlie's grasp. It fell through the railing to the alley below, down two flights of stairs, and landed squarely in a dirty puddle.

Charlie hit me hard in the face, which was a first. I can still remember firsts.

"Max! You little shit!" he said.

It made me feel weird. I thought maybe it would be okay, because in Science class Mr. Frink had told us that the human body consists of sixty percent water, so maybe human leather was the same way, and the glove would be okay.

Charlie brought the glove back into the house and put it in the microwave. I remember the smell of the glove warming, the moistened leather perspiring and crackling at the seams. I still remember firsts. The way he wasn't saying anything to me, which was fine, because I was already too worried about putting human leather into a microwave.

The smell was odd, sort of steaky, like the smell that floated around Sangamon and Racine, by the tanneries, human skin turning over flames. Mr. Frink had assured me that leather wasn't made from human but from animal skin. Both are made of carbon though, so I think I'd rather like to keep the idea of becoming a baseball glove.

The door opened and Dad stepped past me through the doorway. He smelled the way he did on weekends while watching dog races. It seemed out of place. Charlie didn't turn around, but I bet he could feel eyes on his back the way I used to be able to. It was silent for a while, except for the hum of the microwave, and I could feel my chest tightening like a bag of popcorn expanding, filling its spaces. The chimer rang in the air like sonar, like the ones I watch on TV sometimes, in war movies.

"What the hell are you doing?" Dad asked.

Charlie didn't respond. He stood there facing the microwave with his back to both the door and Dad. I wondered if he was starting to lose things, if he forgot how to speak to people, the way I had when Mom died. I wondered if he was becoming like me.

I remember watching Dad grab Charlie's arm and take him into the den, and I remember him closing the door. There was a lot of yelling and other noises. I curled down in the corner of the room outside and covered my ears by the fireplace, next to Leo the Lion, and Grandpa's old slippers. I tried to concentrate on the slippers, because they were made of leather, and I thought maybe I would get lucky and become a pair of slippers. That was the first night I started sleeping with my door open.

Mom died when I was seven, which was three years ago, but I didn't start losing things right away. Our apartment was always cleaner when Mom was around, even though she worked. After Mom was gone, the house stayed clean for a little while. A part of her lingered in the air and crawled along the surfaces of end tables, sitting deep in the cushions of our couches. The house felt the same when I got home from school. I thought maybe a part of us stays behind after we leave for new places. She had been a lawyer, which according to Miss Shelley who teaches English, is someone who puts bad guys in jail, but I didn't like that. Wikipedia says lawyers are people who deliver justice, and I told Miss Shelley that I can understand what it means to deliver justice, and also that Wikipedia is a better teacher than her.

I started losing things after that, after I saw the red around Charlie's eyes, after the house got really dirty and Dad had to hire Nona to make the rooms feel more like Mom, only it wasn't like Mom. That's why I have such trouble with last times. I have too many of them. So I started writing them down in the hidden space behind my bed on the wall. I thought this way I wouldn't forget.

The last time I drank milk was when the power went out, and I couldn't open any more doors, because there weren't any more halls with any more lights to shine in. The last time I played cars was when Charlie didn't come home, because I couldn't crawl into bed with him and I couldn't open any more doors. The last time I combed my hair was when Dad put me to bed and rubbed my head, because his hands smelled like oil and leather, and they reminded me of gloves and slippers. The last time I walked home from school with Charlie, I asked him if he was okay, and the last time I saw him he smelled like Dad.

On my birthday Dad took me camping, and I was excited because Dad was always happy when we went camping, though we hadn't been since before Mom died. We packed Dad's Jeep with everything we would need: a green canvas tent, water, a Dutch Oven, fire starters and matches, Goldfish crackers, sleeping bags, fishing poles, and a harmonica in a leather case, made from some unknown human. Dad slung his canteen over his shoulder and we were off.

It was dark by the time we got to the campsite. Dad had trouble putting up the tent, and he had been forgetting a lot of stuff too, not just our equipment back in the car, but all our old father-son stuff that we used to do. When I was little he used to call out every major city we passed through up into Northern Wisconsin: Sheboygan, Manitowoc, Green Bay, straight on through Gills Rock. We used to play the license plate game, trying to find all fifty states on the road, and I was a champ at that because I found Hawaii. I wanted to pull on Dad's arm to make him stop forgetting; I wanted to tell him that I didn't need help losing more things.

I helped with the fire because I knew how. The other boys who were in Boy Scouts with their dads all knew how and I didn't, so I looked it up on YouTube. I went around looking for wood while Dad lay down on a wool mat by the pit. I scratched my brain, remembering the important thing is to stay away from wood that still has green, because that means it's alive, and living plants consist of anywhere from sixty-five to eighty percent water, like humans, kind of. Then there's construction: smaller pieces at the bottom, bigger ones propped on top. That way air can get through.

The fire was going and we were lying on our mats under the sky – cloudy, no stars, no ghost stories, no Goldfish crackers, and no sleeping bags.

"Dad, are you mad at me?" I asked.

"No, why'd you think that?"

"Are you mad at Charlie?"

"Max, I told you, I'm not mad."

"Can you tell me a ghost story?"

"Bud, I'm tired. Let's just look at the stars. You like stars don't you?"

"Are you mad at Mom?"

"Damn it, Max! I'm not mad."

"But there aren't any stars."

"Then look at the clouds."

He took out the Davy Crockett canteen I gave him for Father's Day three years ago, and he winced when he drank. I asked Mr. Frink about that – why water could make Dad wince, and he told me that sometimes water can get so cold, right before it freezes, that it can feel like it's hot.

By that time I was a year older and I had filled the space behind my bed, so I told Mr. Frink that I wanted to learn new things. I needed to replace the things I had lost. He gave me a book on Astronomy, and I read it three times. I learned that stars are made of hot gas, and that the ones we see in the sky have burnt out long ago. I learned that the planets orbit around the Sun, and that the Hubble Telescope can see hundreds of billions of galaxies like ours, and I thought that people shouldn't be afraid of aliens, because to the aliens we are aliens, and that's a little like being afraid of ourselves. But for as much as I learned from that book, I had filled the inside covers and copyright page and margins with more things I had lost.

The last time I roasted marshmallows we were camping and Dad fell asleep while the fire was still burning, and I stopped peeing in public because, though he was asleep, I was trying to put out the fire. The last time I ate a lollipop was when Nona was cleaning my room because I was afraid she would pull out the bed and see the hidden space on the wall. I was afraid she would see how little of me was left. The last time I watched Ren and Stimpy *was later that night when Dad came home because I thought Nona would tell him about me, but he never said anything.*

Charlie used to do everything with me, even though I was a lot younger. We used to go fishing in the suburbs, and play four-square by the school yard, and he used to show me pictures of girls in magazines. But he didn't say goodbye to me and he hadn't written since he left. It had been months and I hadn't spoken a word to anyone for weeks: not at home, not at school, nowhere. Dad was always working in his study or watching TV. Nona was around, but she spoke funny stuff that I didn't like. I really thought Charlie would send me postcards or stamps or little toys from gas stations. I wanted to know how many miles he had traveled, because his miles were a lot bigger than my miles. He was probably mad at me for having dropped the glove that day. I thought maybe I could cut off my skin to make a new glove, but he had gone where I could not, and I hadn't spoken to anyone.

So I decided to go looking around on the third floor, in Dad's study, where I wasn't allowed to go, searching for my own adventure. As I climbed the staircase in the front entryway, the wooden steps creaked beneath my toes underneath the maroon carpet. There were no pictures on the walls, no landmarks for me to mark my miles. Just a large wooden desk in a sterile room, the only clean room in the house that still felt like Mom. I opened the pen drawer and found tacks, staples, paper clips, and rubber bands. I slammed the drawer shut.

The last time I shot rubber bands the neighbours were having a party. Their music kept me up all night, and outside my window I could hear their front door open and close, open and close.

The other drawers had files in them, papers, yellow legal pads, and a shoebox. Inside the shoebox were pictures of Mom and us, pictures of Grandpa and Dad when he was a kid, pictures of Charlie and me, letters from Mom with Xs and Os, birthday cards, CDs and a Rubik's cube with little words written on each of its tiles, the writing so small and simple, so like my own, and for the first time I wondered if Dad had lost things too.

At the bottom of the drawer was a small envelope with my name on it. It was carelessly torn open, as if the world were running out of time. I pulled the letter out gently, and unfolded it, twice, three times. Charlie had written. The words were his and no one else's. The slow motion of the handwriting had captured his hand, and wrist, and arm. I could hear his voice jump from one line to the next. I didn't know what to do. I wanted to speak, but I couldn't. I wanted to yell; I wanted to run for more than five feet in one single direction, but I was lost.

That night, I couldn't sleep. There were city buses in my ears and clouds in the ceiling blocking out my glow-in-the-dark stars. I rolled out of my sheets and got into Charlie's bed. Under the covers it still felt like

Charlie hadn't left, the way Dad's study still felt like Mom. I pulled away the pillows and checked the wall behind his bed.

Kimberly Gibson

Believer

The subway rocks our bodies like our cradles once did. There are no more first words to be learned and nowhere for the preacher's words to go. Our minds are full and silent. We are busy people occupying the same space, giving up seats for the weak amongst us, taking this brief time to breathe. We try to be conscious of nothing in the world but ourselves and our stops, but we notice her and avert our eyes.

The preacher's thin lips part as she looks not at us, but right above our heads. Dark brown curls cover her blue eyes and she pulls her hand through her thick strands, while gripping the Bible in her other hand. She is wearing a button-down floral shirt with white lace around the shoulders and khaki pants. Her skin is clear and flushed and if she hadn't opened her mouth, we might have thought she was a commuter like us.

She doesn't see the woman in front of her with the long auburn hair, pale skin, and fixed brown eyes. The preacher passes her and brushes a teenage boy's jeans. He presses his legs into the dividing panel. As she walks by each of us, some of us bury our faces in our newspapers, while the rest of us read over our neighbour's shoulder. We turn up our headphones and think with a louder inner voice.

The preacher changes her tone.

She says, "You must walk in love, walk in faith! None of you take the time to live or even think about values anymore. If you don't change your ways, you could end up down below!" We feel her breeze past us with her quick, rough steps. She stops and grabs hold of the pole, blocking a woman in the seat before her. The woman is looking at her green eyes in her hand mirror, but the preacher's elbow blocks her view. The woman shakes her head in anger. We know she wants to say something, but won't. The preacher continues, "When was the last time you had dinner with your family and held hands around the dinner table together and prayed? Jesus performed mighty deeds, saved your souls, and you can't even thank him before you take a bite to eat? Take out, that's all you want. The TV and Internet ruin your minds and your relationships. The only book that needs to be read is the Bible. Do you understand? I'm telling you to look above and see what kind of life you could have without these distractions!"

Some of us secretly love killing the hour with her company. She will give us something to talk about with our co-workers. Our chests jerk and we laugh out of our noses. Others feel sorry for her. Yet we are still getting to where we need to be. There are still a few moments before work. We can use this time to clean our glasses, check for split ends, or do nothing at all. Some days it is enough just to sit in the first seat and look out at the tunnel ahead.

We let the preacher go on about how the world is under judgment because her outrage isn't surprising. But then the preacher begins to pace faster and speak louder. Her pacing turns into a frantic dance. She calls for someone to join her. No one does. There would be a different outcome if it were the late night train with the bar crowd, but we won't react. An older man leans his elbow on his knee and runs his hand along his smooth chin as the preacher passes him. A young girl bends down and digs through her plastic shopping bag, full of books, topped off with a pair of high heels. No one invites eye contact. The preacher stops in the middle of the subway car, hunches over and smiles.

Bursting into action, she rushes towards a man leaning against the doors. He wears a slicked back ponytail and a dark grey suit. She walks towards him with faith on her shoulders and says to the ceiling, "God loves you if you believe." As she reaches him, she trips over his expensive shoes. We bite our lips as she stumbles, grabbing frantically for something to help her regain balance, but it is no use; the preacher falls into the woman next to him. This woman has a fierce, round face outlined in flawless makeup. She doesn't even flinch as the preacher's weight falls into her plump stomach. She catches the preacher's arm and takes a step back, while wiping off her pressed black trousers. She is an experienced commuter; her *Wall Street Journal* is folded to perfection, she stands straight in high heels and she isn't fazed by a clumsy passenger. The preacher, struggling back to her feet, turns to her and says, "I'll ask you one question. Do you believe?"

"That's enough," the woman says instantly. She has a serious, flat mouth.

The preacher continues pressing and we are no longer ashamed to stare. Our newspapers rest on our fingertips and fall to our laps and we keep the headphones in, but pause the music. The train is approaching the second to last stop and the preacher begins to speak more urgently and her hands begin to quiver. She focuses on the woman with the fierce face, extends her arm and shows her the Bible. She says, "So many things go wrong in life, but faith is the one thing we have that will never go bad."

The woman rolls her eyes.

"Don't you agree?" asks the preacher.

The woman says bluntly, "No." Our eyes stare so intently, it is as if we are elbowing each other for a good view.

The preacher asks, "Then what do you believe?" We put our heads down, but our eyes watch incredulously. Many of us think she should consider herself lucky no one has said anything to her before this. Yet we worry that we hate this woman. We fear that we are anti-religion. But some of us went to church on Sunday. Some of us go once a year and hate her for reminding us. Some of us silently say a prayer to convince whatever we believe in that we still believe. Some of us don't care and resent this woman because we didn't get to finish preparing for work, didn't get to read that newspaper story, and for causing us to crave a cigarette ten minutes earlier than usual.

The preacher's smile fades and she speaks harshly. "Are you a Jew?" The fierce-faced woman gives her no reaction. "A Hindu? A Buddhist? A Pagan?" We no longer feel sorry for hating her. Her voice speaks each word with such disdain and cynical articulation that we want to grab her face, ask her to look straight at us and tell her to shut up. "A Taoist? A Muslim?" The preacher mispronounces Taoist, with extra emphasis on a T sound, and we hate her for making us hate the subway. She reminds us how many breakfasts we miss, how much we sweat and how much time we spend in these cars.

She turns in a circle and gazes at each of us, searching for our faces for the first time. She looks to a homeless man and he averts his eyes and looks down at his boots stained with white water marks. An attractive woman uses the subway's glass as a vanity to paint her lips before the preacher's eyes can approach her. We do our best to ignore the preacher, but can't help looking out the corner of our eyes. She stops and asks, "Do you all think you were self-made? You need to thank your creator every day."

She is asking us to care in the one part of our day where we don't have to. This is the one part of the day where we don't need to have fake conversations; we don't need to talk about the weather while in the elevator; we don't need to listen to the guy at work who picks his nose while telling you a story. We don't need to think about those serious conversations either. We don't need to think about how to tell our spouses we fantasise about seeing other people, we don't need to tell our kids why their classmate is sick, and we don't need to discuss why we are here. This is the part of our day where we are quiet and sit closer to strangers than we sometimes sit next to our closest friends. This is the part of our day where we don't need to pry, where we don't need to know what the person across from us is going through. This preacher is asking us to think, to speak up and in a subway car our conflicts don't have anything to do but collide.

The woman with the fierce face opens her mouth and says, "Actually." Her voice breaks the silence and falls over the car. We watch her closely, as if she is about to kick a field goal and if she misses we'll lose the championship. "I believe that without a god we'd be okay with just each other." We don't expect it. We are still and the preacher squints at her. For a few seconds, all we hear is the preacher's gold ring banging against the pole and an announcement that we are arriving at the next stop.

Someone claps.

The preacher takes her Bible and presses it against the fierce-faced woman's chest. She says, "Sit down! I am holy! You can be holy too!"

"Okay, okay. Step away," yells the woman with the fierce face. As the double doors of the subway open, the woman pushes the Bible off her chest and out of the preacher's hands. The book slams onto the ground and slides out of the subway car. We cringe. The Bible has gold edges, hard black binding and is larger than the average commuter paperback. The preacher falls to her knees and crawls out of the subway car, scrambling after her book. People shuffle around her as they exit and enter the train. The crowd blocks her view of the Bible and she tries to keep her hands firmly on the ground to feel for the tome. As sharp heels and rubber soles hit the ground, she is forced to lift her hands and sit back on her knees. The doors begin to ring and the preacher remains frozen on the platform. A part of her ankle shows under her khaki pants and her skin is dry and bleached white. Her head shakes quickly as the doors begin to close. She mutters frantically and looks at us as if it is important we understand. Her body makes slow progress towards her Bible, and her khaki pants, now stained with filth, are slowly covered by the metal doors as they shut, quieting the subway car.

The fierce-faced woman opens her mouth. "I'm..." she begins, but chooses not to complete her sentence.

The preacher's words weigh down on our chests. We sit silently for a while in a meditative state. We could spend hours like that, not talking. But some of us think: *Good riddance*. Some of us even say it under our breath.

The train slows down and we all stand up to leave. Before the doors open, we catch each others' eyes and we nod as if to say, "Take care; I'll be back soon." The fierce-faced woman takes a second look at us. As the train's pulse stops, we begin to walk forward, but the doors stay closed. We wait and appreciate this moment for forcing us to slow down. The doors open. Things start moving again. We go our separate ways.

Ryan Huntley

Standing in Sandy's Driveway

I.

I've had a cracked, smoke-amber doorknob in my jacket pocket for days.
If it was attached to the front door of the house you grew
up in with your mother, I could have found it ironic
that its ruined, punched-in beauty was so similar to your eyes.

II.

Itinerant between the kitchen table and back door;
the snow hadn't yet curtained your gazing window.
Soon, in sweeps, winter will bring out the rabbit and deer
footprints that you trail between each morning, smiling.

III.

Stars patchwork a labyrinth and at the same time are our guide.
Casting about the power lines that hang over the house
you never loved or could learn to hold, our pines would go
on for days until they reached the farmhouse where coyotes
ripped open chickens, and plain left
to wander snow dusted, cracked down corn.

IV.

Your sad carpet of clothes cover scuffed-floorboard
scars from dragging chairs to hang photographs.
Weathered by swaying maple leaves that got in

through the window never fixed, that screen door your mother forgot to latch,
your quilts hang damp over chair backs every breakfast.

V.

Cradling your novels and parakeet –
the sun began to sag and fluorescent peach
spread a wildfire along the back porch,
in through the window and screen door, illuminating
the patient, empty dinner plates. When no one came home
I came over and we made popcorn and a phone call.

VI.

The transmigration of your soul won't happen
again this year. One day, holidays won't mean
taking out the recycling at night to protect
the dirty, pink elephant that sleeps upstairs.
One day, your mother's car will be parked
as straight as a highway and your heart
won't burn like a long line of desert fires.

Reverberation

There is something past the salt-sprayed rocks buoyantly keeping breath
with the sea. Afternoon strollers and dog runners stop
beside me and we squint together, not trusting our sun-spot eyes.

True, it's overcast by a dripping barge that slowly drags
itself south along the coast, and the glare isn't helping anyone –
but there is a silhouetted swan quietly faring January's waves.

Its reverie-head is slender and tucked half behind its left wing.
Rustling ever so faintly, a lazy lilac that winter forgot –
close-eyed and fantasising, whether or not to disarm its situation.

We stand along the quay as the hauler's destination is kept.
Its passing deck rails cause zoetrope bars of light that break lovely
across the silty water and spin a thousand pictures behind my eyes.

I can't help but imagine which one of us is the bird, barge, or tide.
I think about the quaint ruffle of books and papers
that sleep beside me and how I tell myself each time I'm curled
in that feathery reverb of sheets that they should be you –
your hair thoroughly messed by dreams and by me.
I've chosen for you the ineffable Greystones' sky,
and for myself, the decidedly swan-cradling sea.

In the Neighbourhood, Again

Covering our lights with a sheet
and faces with plastic,
we follow the creased map that time
stained upon the backs of our hands.
Bound to gravel driveways –
an inverted sky raging thunderclouds
and snarling – we're skinny little red
heat lightning out across the neighbourhood.
Feeling like the moon emptying
down onto a vacant building lot,
with a king-size candy wrapper
someone staunches the wound
that a low hanging branch left
on their soft, right cheek.
Some of us are too tall for this.
Spookadelic booberry punch
and Riggy says he'll never cover
himself in toilet paper again
unless he's drunk in the bathroom.

And the masquerade ball used to take
shape as silhouetted children darted
between hedgerows and fences
until midnight came and nobody
was foolish enough to open their doors.
Jamie Lee's sister, KristieJo, dressed
like between a prostitute and a firefighter

and we were too young to really know
what to say or what to stare at so we blew cold
breath at our sneakers and jammed candy corn
far back into our mouths and chewed awfully
quickly.

The Blue Marlin Motel

electric blue-wire light fish

static over the rooftops

on 1320 Simonton Street

casts a deep ocean

wave all over the sidewalks

while the street's getting ready

for Thursday night feet

and the parking meters

just begin to weep

and bend

towards that lightning fish

hovering alone over the palms

The Scaffolding, The Night Rain

The Moon: still learning to part brick-coloured
light pollution clouds that shift and shudder
behind a stream of shelter-determined rainbirds.
I will learn by heart the blueness and knots
that glaze and twine over the scaffolding
outside my window; I will climb out onto the landing
of this organic crosshatching and run my asphalt-wound hands
across each inch. I step outside and greet the weather
while making it back indoors with dry feet.

Silence: in it, the only realisation, the wind.
The wind hushes everything while vibrating elevator cables,
causing rain to stammer one-side, encroaching
through ventilator ducts that writhe discomforts.
I don't ask much, but to find what offers itself
then escapes me: a conversation composed with the ungraspable
evening that amounts to everything, a warm hand
slipped tightly between mine while our eyes watch all this.

Tonight: no-celebration. My reflection,
the inverse of a party hat – a funeral shroud, sops
up the Christmas rain while I pick a minuscule
street pebble out of my palm, and bleed some.

A Letter to a Desk from Virginia

You're scratched all over
and I wonder who keyed their name
straight into the grain of your walnut face.

I've spent my nights battling a mattress
and, once again, convincing myself that I'm down
in New Orleans while Death, solidified in dreams
and laughter, peers rum drunk over the galleries;
half-dressed with wet, red lips and sediment-sprayed thighs.
I'm superstitious of my eyes and my chest pounds
like hail bouncing off a drum. I don't know
her at all, but I miss her and so what?

So what, I place the cobalt dream stone at the bottom
of a voodoo water glass by my head –
a song that I play on the hushed keys in my mouth.
I ask the piano to play that left hand of his –
the one that rattles between my heavy bones and sorrow.
When he did, all the poppies outside the gallery bloomed.
The sky forced its red day-ending all over
the stained buildings and everyone opened
their door-sized shutters for the evening.
I asked the lamppost shadows to take
each and every hallway and make them hum
smeared electric tangerine onto the streets.
The power lines above my head bled together
and formed scripture that fluttered off when trash scattered past.

The water drowns under the canal-bound fog.
The fences endure the roar of crickets.
The washed out Spanish moss drips off the morning.
"Marie" is spray-painted on a grave
and that is all that made it past the flood.
That old fan hanging from her gallery is broken,
but its spirit still rolls and I feel no breeze.
Out on Jackson Avenue purple beads
hang off the street signs and trolleys
break down because cars do not break fast enough.
Relatives drape purple, green and gold
from family graves, but someone got buried
in 2002 and no one strung any beads up for him.

Azaleas grow beside a barricaded bridge.
This morning the interstate drifts heavy and slow.
Beside a downed cab on the highway,
concrete pillars are so drowned out
they have taught themselves to rot.
Azrael, standing quiet next to a pale sage horse,
waits with ten thousand tongues
as Gabriel goes gallery to cast iron gallery
delivering the news.
Still all the bayou azaleas bloom.
Still the trumpets fold.

You're scratched all over
and I wonder who keyed "Caroline"
straight into the grain of your walnut face.

About the Authors

Sara Baume was born in Wigan in 1984, and grew up in Cork. She graduated with a B.A. in Fine Art in 2007. She has since published interviews, articles and reviews on visual art, and has crafted many kinetic sculptures and multimedia installations. She is mostly based in Dublin and can be found at www.sarabaume.wordpress.com.

Catherine Finn is originally from Wexford and now lives in Dublin. She has a B.Sc in Communications and Journalism and has had fiction published in *The Stinging Fly*.

Kimberly Gibson grew up in New Jersey and has lived in Boston, Galway, and Dublin. She studied English Literature and Creative Writing at Montclair State University and attended the International Writers Program at National University of Ireland, Galway. She writes fiction and is currently working on a collection of short stories.

Eleanor Hooker began her career as a nurse and midwife. She later achieved a B.A. (Hons 1st) from the Open University and an M.A. (Hons) in Cultural History from the University of Northumbria. Eleanor is Helm and Press Officer for Lough Derg RNLI (Royal National Lifeboat Institution) Lifeboat, and a founding member of the Dromineer Literary Festival. She lives in North Tipperary and is working towards her first poetry collection.

Ryan Huntley grew up in Pennsylvania and lives in New York City. He studied Creative Writing and Literature at the New School for Liberal Arts. He writes poetry and fiction.

Darren David Koolman was born on the island of Aruba in 1981 to an Irish mother and Dutch father. He moved to Ireland in 1991 and has lived there ever since. He is an aspiring poet, and attributes his love of literature to his upbringing in the land of saints and scholars.

Steven Louie was born in Maryland in 1985, but considers Chicago his home. He earned his Bachelor's degree in English Literature and Creative Writing from the University of Illinois, focusing primarily on poetry and short fiction. He will be attending the Medill School of Journalism at Northwestern University in 2010.

Eddie Naessens graduated in Philosophy from Trinity College Dublin in 2009 and is also a comedian, actor, and a qualified software engineer. He was nominated for a Smedia Award in 2008 for his first published short story. He grew up in Wexford and lives in Dublin with his lovable wife and son.

Annemarie Ní Churreáin is originally from Donegal and has lived in Dublin and India. In 2001, she graduated from Dublin City University with a B.A. in Communication Studies. She has written for stage, screen, gallery exhibitions and print publications. She is currently working towards completion of her first poetry collection.

Maura Amy Roosevelt grew up in Cambridge, Massachusetts and graduated from Harvard University in 2007. She worked in the publishing industry in New York City before studying in Dublin. Maura is currently working on a novel, and in the fall of 2010 she will begin the MFA programme at New York University.

David Rowell was a prize-winner in the Swift Satire, Goldsmith, Amergin, Golden Pen and Francis Ledwidge poetry competitions. He has published in *Poetry Ireland Review, Crannog Magazine, Authors and Artists, Living It, Gates of Ivory and Horn, and County Lines*. He read in Poetry Ireland's *Introduction* series. His prose pieces have been broadcasted on RTÉ and RTÉ Lyric FM.

Eva Sandoval is a New York University graduate. She was born in Boston, grew up in Florida, and calls New York City home. Before studying in Dublin, she lived in Japan for two years. Her parents are from Italy and Guatemala. Eva likes to write about all these places. She has been an editor, a critic, and a travel writer. She is writing a novel.

Anna Smith was raised on Canada's West Coast and is a graduate of the University of Victoria's Creative Writing Program. When not writing, Anna fences for Canada and Ireland.

The contact information for all authors can be found at
www.leaveussomeunreality.wordpress.com
Alternatively, you can email owc.anthology@gmail.com